MARKETING ETHICS

MARKETING ETHICS

Rick D. Saucier

With a Preface by
Kimberly K. Folkers

The Edwin Mellen Press
Lewiston•Queenston•Lampeter

Library of Congress Cataloging-in-Publication Data

Saucier, Rick D.
  Marketing ethics / Rick D. Saucier ; with a preface by Kimberly K. Folkers.
    p. cm.
  Includes bibliographical references and index.
  ISBN-13: 978-0-7734-5116-2
  ISBN-10: 0-7734-5116-1
  1. Marketing--Moral and ethical aspects. 2. Advertising--Moral and ethical aspects.
I. Title.
174.9'381 2008
9780773451162--dc22

                                                2008299406

hors série.

A CIP catalog record for this book is available from the British Library.

The Edwin Mellen Press	The Edwin Mellen Press
Box 450	Box 67
Lewiston, New York	Queenston, Ontario
USA 14092-0450	CANADA L0S 1L0

The Edwin Mellen Press, Ltd.
Lampeter, Ceredigion, Wales
UNITED KINGDOM SA48 8LT

Printed in the United States of America

To Emily, my personal experience in consumer behavior education

TABLE OF CONTENTS

LIST OF EXHIBITS

Preface

Today's marketing environment is more complex than ever. Consumers have unprecedented choices and easy access to many of the companies offering these choices, but are also increasingly cynical about the messages and marketing approaches intended to inform them of these choices. Consumers long for meaningful relationships with organizations of integrity that understand their needs and wants, but resist many marketing efforts intended to establish these connections. Marketers face the unique challenge of making sense of these apparent contradictions as they work to build relationships with their customers. Unfortunately, they sometimes resort to less than ethical methods in their attempts to break through the clutter to connect with consumers and reach them with persuasive messages.

This book addresses some of the key ethical concerns related to marketing and advertising practices. It focuses attention on the nature of new ethical breaches made possible by the increasing capabilities of technology, and revisits some of the classic ethical missteps that have been made in marketing over the years. Its examination of marketing ethics comes at a particularly strategic time for marketers and students of marketing. The 2005 Marketing Receptivity Survey done by Yankelovich Partners, Inc., cites several disturbing findings. First that "the classic approach to marketing is rapidly vanishing from the scene," second, that "the biggest challenge facing marketers is not the appearance of new media, but the disappearance of engaged, receptive audiences," and third, that "the chief reason for marketing resistance is the level of saturation and intrusiveness that characterizes the contemporary consumer experience with marketing." (Yankelovich Partners, Inc., 2005)

In Trust in Advertising, it is noted that new digital channels such as the Internet and mobile phones, are very scalable, providing more cost effective ways than ever to reach very targeted audiences. However, as they also point out, the result of this appealing cost effectiveness is a temptation to abuse or at least overuse these new channels. (A.C. Nielsen, 2007)

These findings reveal a serious dilemma that impacts almost every ethical issue raised in this book. As marketers look for new and better approaches to marketing, they are faced with the realization that the very consumers they wish to reach - consumers who are eager for meaningful connections with companies and organizations - are also potentially the same consumers who are increasingly disengaged from the marketplace and resistant to being approached. Often their resistance is the result of what they have come to view as an intrusive and sometimes unethical marketing environment.

Whatever new model of marketing emerges in coming years, it must have at its center a renewed commitment to marketing ethics. It is only when consumers are convinced beyond a reasonable doubt that marketers are treating them respectfully and ethically that they will consider opening themselves to marketing advances. Consumers must be able to trust the companies they do business with and ideally, over time begin to believe that the marketing profession as a whole is doing everything possible to make unethical marketing a thing of the past.

This view seems to be confirmed in the Yankelovich study. "Consumers are unwilling to spend time with marketing that doesn't measure up. Not only is such marketing ineffective, consumers view it as a bad experience with the brands." (Yankelovich, 2005) If the marketing not only does not measure up, but deteriorates further into unethical practices, the negativity toward the brand and potentially the overall field of marketing will be even more severe. Organizations must realize that "marketing itself is now a brand attribute and benefit" that consumers will evaluate. (Yankelovich, 2005) A solid understanding of ethical marketing practices is absolutely essential in this environment.

Finally, in the article "Making the Perfect Marketer," it seems clear that "the marketing function is more important than ever before" with marketing being increasingly essential to corporate success. (Hyde, Landry, and Tipping, 2004) Marketers must embrace their role as key players in the success of their organizations. This vital role must be carried out with a clear understanding of and commitment to the very best in ethical marketing practices. As Saucier points out throughout this book, the field of marketing must seriously focus on dispelling the notion that "marketing ethics is a contradiction in terms."

Kimberly K. Folkers
Associate Professor of Marketing
Wartburg College

References:

A.C. Nielsen (2007). Trust in Advertising: A Global Nielsen Consumer Report. *http://www.nielsen.com.*

Hyde, P., Landry, E., and Tipping, A. (2004). Making the Perfect Marketer. *Strategy+Business, Winter 2004.*

Yankelovich Partners, Inc. (2005). 2005 Marketing Receptivity Survey: A Yankelovich MONITOR Omniplus Study – Topline Report.

Foreword

An Overview of Marketing Ethics

I can still remember how different marketing was a generation ago. I remember as a young child going to the local convenience store to buy candy cigarettes that made me feel grown up. Life seemed simple - three television networks were on the air and no internet or cell phone technology existed. Certainly people seemed to live simpler in modest homes. Privacy issues only arose if someone listened in on your party phone line. The world seemed more safe and secure. School was a haven from the world. Growing up before Twiggy became the rage as a model (and made the waif look in vogue), girls didn't feel so much pressure to be skinny.

My students today live in a much different world – one that is fast paced with constant pressure to buy products and services that will allow them to conform to society's norms that are often dictated by the American media and the marketing profession.

At the beginning of a semester, I like to start my consumer behavior course by asking my students if they believe that consumers can control their decisions or if they have self will to resist marketing messages aimed at them. A discussion on consumer freedom quickly ensues and is at the heart of any discussion on marketing ethics. Of course, most students like to believe they have total control on their consuming decisions. As the semester progresses, some, if not most of the class start to change their mind once they see for themselves the cognitive and emotional techniques used by the marketing profession to influence consumers.

If the United States truly has a capitalist free-market economy, then competition between companies should focus on product innovation and constant quality improvement. Under free market conditions, a company's marketing efforts should be directed to fully informing and persuading consumers in their target market as to why consumers should choose their product over the competitor's.

This scenario sounds great until one considers the relative ability of consumers to be fully knowledgeable in the choices they face. My students quickly discover that while consumers have access to sources of information undreamed of a generation ago, many consumers still rely too often on the information that companies choose to provide. Unfortunately, not all businesses operate in an ethical manner.

Another issue with a free-market economy where consumers can exercise total control over their decisions is the assumption that consumers are rational by nature. Most students strongly believe that they have free will and can self determine their behaviors and consumer decisions and they do so in a rational manner. While there is still much research that needs to be done to better understand how consumers react to emotional appeals, no doubt exists as to the power of using emotions in advertising to overcome cognitive arguments that take place in consumers' minds.

To better understand and explore consumer decision making, I decided to add a component to the consumer behavior course designed to encourage students to delve deeper into marketing's ethical role in influencing consumer free will. So I looked at many of the widespread controversial ethical issues that appear most relevant to the current times. Marketers are using many types of fear tactics to scare consumers to purchase their products or change their behaviors. Marketers are intruding into our lives at escalating levels. Is there any sanctuary from all the advertising constantly bombarding us? Interestingly, one of the hot topics in the marketing profession is how to use guerilla tactics to reach consumers who are becoming more and more turned off from all the advertising constantly pitched at them. A particularly controversial concern is the emotional appeals directed at children who often cannot separate fantasy from reality. These appeals sometimes manipulate children who in turn manipulate their parents. On another note, marketers have learned to push people's emotional buttons to make them feel inadequate and that the only way to feel better is to spend money (that they sometimes don't have) to purchase product they often don't need. Sadly, too often these purchases don't address the most important needs that people feel. As a consequence, people enter into a spiral of spending that never adequately addresses their needs. In the meantime, all the consumer purchases encourage unnecessary debt and create harm to our environment. A different issue has arisen from marketers employing models that promote unhealthy body images. For women, a super thin, or waif look, may promote eating disorders and depression while male models reflect an Adonis look which may be only attainable through using steroids that can harm young men's bodies. Another hot topic that consumers, companies, and legislators are trying to come to grips with is managing individuals' privacy. How much information should an organization be allowed to gather and what obligatory safeguards should be in place? This issue was powerfully demonstrated to me one class when a panel of students showed all the information they were able to gather on me simply by obtaining my phone number and address from the public phone book. The most recent issue our class has discussed is the modern use of puffery. The discussion usually delves into the issue of what point does puffing your product become deceptive? The answer becomes difficult to pin down and not surprisingly students find that while a few vague guidelines exist, one judges puffery claims on a case by case basis.

A student panel is placed in charge of a class period to lead a discussion on each of these issues. In all these discussions, students often learn legal and industry standards do not always exist and that they must apply their values in order to resolve these ethical issues. Along the way, they find that they may not be able to avail themselves of free choice because of the strong influence marketers bring to bear on their consuming decisions.

This work is not meant to address all marketing ethical issues, but rather those that are currently under particular scrutiny and affects common practices that are widespread through out the industry. As the profession continues to evolve and self examines their practices, new issues may arise or move to the forefront of the discussion. Today's undergraduate marketing students will find that the issues raised in this book may allow them to be better prepared for the challenges they face in their careers.

ACKNOWLEDGMENTS

Many people provided invaluable contributions and support that allowed me to complete this work. I'm especially thankful for the loving support and proofreading by my wife, Debbie. My colleagues at the College of St. Benedict and St. John's University have encouraged my scholarly efforts ever since my arrival at the respective colleges. I am grateful for your encouragement. Sue Zimmer, my department's administrative assistant helped with word processing sections of this study. Finally, special thanks go out to my Marketing Management Association colleagues who helped to read, critique, and provide guidance:

Mary Albrecht, Maryville University

Nora Ganim Barnes, University of Massachusetts

Kim Folkers, Wartburg College

Fred Hoyt, Illinois Wesleyan University

Dena Lieberman, Alverno College

Lisa Lindgren, St. John's University

Lori Lohman, Augsburg College

Chapter 1

Marketing Ethics: A Discussion

"Always do right – this will gratify some and astonish the rest"

- Mark Twain

What is Marketing Ethics?

Marketing ethics is often viewed as a contradiction in terms. Because marketing represents the most visible part of an organization, people especially view marketing with cynicism. But how can a business promote products effectively in a highly competitive world without resorting to highly questionable tactics? The pressure to achieve short term financial gains may lead management to consider pursuing problematic strategies that while legal, create stakeholder issues with respect to perceived values of honesty, respect, and fairness. The Ethics Resource Center's most recent National Business Ethics Survey reported that 52% of employees observed at least one type of misconduct in the past year. So how does an organization ethically conduct business in a profitable manner?

A discussion of contemporary ethical marketing issues in America begins with a common understanding of what is meant by the term ethics. The American Marketing Association defines marketing ethics as:

"Standards of marketing decision making based on 'what is right' and 'what is wrong,' and emanating from our religious heritage and our traditions of social, political, and economic freedom. The use of moral codes, values, and standards to determine whether marketing actions are good or evil, right or wrong. Often standards are based on professional or association codes of ethics. (Marketing Terms Dictionary, 2007)

1

Paul Taylor, Emeritus Professor of Philosophy at Brooklyn College City University of New York, defines ethics as an "inquiry into the nature and grounds of morality where the term morality is taken to mean moral judgments, standards, and rules of conduct." (Taylor, 1975)

Taken together, ethics appear to incorporate an individual's morals and values to create standards and rules to form judgments on what represents proper conduct. Moral standards regard behavior that is of serious consequence to human welfare that can profoundly injure or benefit people. (Velasquez, 2006) Good moral principals suggest that we should treat one another with dignity and respect. This in turn suggests that moral standards should take priority over self-interest. Furthermore, the validity of moral standards depends not on a particular group's authority but rather on quality of life arguments. (Shaw & Barry, 2007)

Marketing Ethics and Social Responsibility

An understanding of marketing ethics must also consider the social responsibility or an organization's obligation to the society in which it conducts business. Social responsibilities include economic, legal, and philanthropic responsibilities. A business must produce goods and services that society needs and wants at a reasonable price that satisfies the marketplace, can sustain the business, and satisfy the investors. An organization must follow the laws in the geographic areas it operates. Ethical responsibilities encompass the behaviors and activities of the organization as expected by society but are not codified into law. Philanthropic responsibilities are best represented through behaviors and activities that society desires. Social responsibility then can best be seen as moving beyond economic and legal obligations in order to reach an understanding with the society in which the organization operates. Business ethics and social responsibility together provide a foundation on how to best conduct business decisions to satisfy the environment in which the organization conducts its business. (Carroll, 1989)

2

At times, individuals may encounter difficulties distinguishing between the legal and ethical arena. Many laws exist which an organization is obligated to obey. The United States federal government has created many laws that protect consumers such as the Pure Food and Drug Act of 1906, the Fair Credit Billing Act of 1974, and the Children's Online Privacy Protection Act of 1998. At times ethical issues may be decided through a civil suit in a court of law. One way to distinguish between a legal and an ethical decision is at the point when legal rules no longer provide a framework for arriving at a decision and one is faced with using their values and moral standards to arrive at a judgment regarding a situation one has never faced before. If an individual or organization view a decision as acceptable, but society does not, the organization must still hold itself accountable for its actions. If enough public resistance or outcry develops, legislation may be enacted that restricts or bans a specific business practice. In 1991, the United States Congress approved the Federal Sentencing Guidelines for Organizations. The Guidelines codified into law incentives for organizations to take action to prevent misconduct, such as developing effective internal ethical compliance programs. (Conaboy, 1995)

Ethical and social responsibilities depend on the values and principles held by individuals and groups both inside and outside of an organization. The values and moral beliefs of key stakeholders such as owners, investors, top management, employees, customers, and the community at large all interact in a social and economics framework. For effective ethical leadership to occur, top management must create a meaningful dialogue between stakeholders and society that assess and addresses these ethical issues in order to resolve conflicts. Organizations tend to reflect the values and standards of their top management team. Management leadership therefore must serve as role models for all members of the organization through their demonstration of effective ethical behavior.

3

Ethical Conflict

Ethical issues often emerge when conflicting goals arise between stakeholders of an organization. Stakeholders' conflicting interests may appear at times to present top leadership with a daunting task. A common perspective suggests that attempting to respect all stakeholders' rights may often limit management's ability to maximize shareholder value. Marketing theory states the opposite. An over emphasis on addressing the needs of the shareholder may result in undervaluing the company's customers. When a company puts forth in good faith its best efforts to concentrate on the needs of the customer in a morally respectful manner, the business will achieve their appropriate financial rewards, creating a situation where the customers, shareholders, and society all win. (Shaw & Barry, 2007)

To create this environment where everyone wins is not easy. Ethical challenges may arise from a number of sources. The greater the perceived relevance and importance of the issue the greater the ethical intensity can become. Severe competition may make managers feel that their organization's survival is threatened. In this type of situation managers may see previously unacceptable alternatives as acceptable and start to engage in questionable practices, rationalizing the actions chosen as necessary for the company to survive. One easy example is that profit is a main goal for most corporations. To achieve this goal top management often sets financial objectives such as market share and return on equity. America's shareholder fixation with short-term performance adds extra pressure for top management. Many times an ethical dilemma may arise from a conflict between a financial goal and an action that may not be perceived as being in the best interests of society. Corporate financial goals are often broken down into individual goals upon which performance is measured and financial rewards given. Ethical issues arise when managers experience conflict in their decisions because of excessive pressure from top leadership to meet their goals. In one survey 50 percent of top managers, 65 percent of middle managers, and 84 percent of lower managers today feel under

4

pressure to compromise personal standards to achieve company goals. (Snoeyenbos, Almeder, & Humber, 2001)

If marketing involves persuading customers of a need for the organization's product or service, then marketers must examine the ethical aspects of what is involved when they are pressured to influence a consumer's behavior and decision making in an unethical manner. For example, two forms of persuasion most would consider unethical include manipulation and coercion. Kathleen Kelley Reardon describes manipulation as:

> "...furthering a person's or organizational goals at the expense of the person being manipulated. It essentially involves 'pulling the wool over the eyes' of others. The person being manipulated are not encouraged to reason about the situation, but are entranced by false promises, deceived by insincere verbal or nonverbal behaviors, or 'set up' in the sense that the situation is contrived to limit their choices. Manipulation differs from persuasion by robbing people of their choices through deceptive tactics, rather than attempt to guide them to make, of their own free will, the persuader's preferred choice."

She goes on to describe coercion as "involving physical force or some form of threat." (Reardon, 1991)

Some managers compromise their ethics by viewing business as a game. The author of "Is Business Bluffing Ethical" suggests that these managers view this game as impersonal with rules that are different from the rest of society. Moral standards most people would question may become acceptable in the business world because the managers involved are only playing a game and no one really gets hurt. The problem is that many members of society do not consciously and freely choose to play in the game. By divorcing business from reality, managers may act as if everyday business activity has nothing to do with society's standards of morality. (Carr, 1968)

If one must think of ethics as a game, Shaw and Barry in the tenth edition of "Moral Issues in Business" suggest the following rules:

5

1. Consider other people's well being, including the well being of non-participants.
2. Think as a member of the business community and not as an isolated individual.
3. Obey, but do not depend solely on the law.
4. Think of yourself – and your company – as part of society.
5. Obey moral rules.
6. Think objectively.
7. Ask yourself "What kind of person would do such a thing?" (Shaw & Barry, 2007)

In 2004, the American Marketing Association (AMA) arrived at their own set of game rules through an updated code of ethics entitled: "Ethical Norms and Values for Marketers." The entire AMA Code of Ethics is reproduced in the Appendix. The code focuses on norms and values that represent the most significant criteria to evaluate the actions of marketing practitioners. The norms include "do no harm, foster trust, and practice fundamental ethical values that will improve consumer confidence in the integrity of the marketing exchange system." Implicitly stated, marketers must accomplish these norms through building relationships with integrity and good faith through marketing communications that are not intentionally deceptive or misleading. To accomplish this commitment, the AMA Code of Conduct recommends that organizations adopt six key values:

1. Honesty – to be truthful and forthright in dealings with customers and stakeholders.
2. Responsibility – to accept the consequences of marketing decisions and strategies
3. Fairness – to try to balance the needs of the buyer with the interest of the seller.

4. Respect – to acknowledge the basic human dignity of all stakeholders.

5. Openness – to create transparency in our marketing operations.

6. Citizenship – to fulfill the economic, legal, philanthropic and societal responsibilities that serve stakeholders in a strategic manner. (AMA Updates Association's Code of Ethics, 2004)

The American Marketing Association defines marketing as "an organizational function and a set of processes for creating, communicating, and delivering value to customers and for managing customer relationships in such ways that benefit organizations and stakeholders. (Marketing Terms Dictionary, 2007) An organization's relationship with its customers and stakeholders will not be mutually beneficial if one or both parties don't respect the other and if an agreement is not entered into voluntarily. Customers must freely consent to the relationship and be fully informed of the condition of that relationship.

As William Shaw and Vincent Barry so aptly point out, "Business ethics begins with consumer demand and productivity, with the freedom to engage in business as one wishes, and with the hope – inconceivable in most parts of the world – that one can better one's life considerably through one's own hard work and intelligence." They go on to suggest that this statement represents the underpinnings of the values of business ethics – "To define and defend the basic goals of prosperity, freedom, fairness, and individual dignity." As such, individuals need to recognize both intended and unintended consequences of their actions on people and groups both inside and outside the organization. (Shaw & Barry, 2007) If organizations strive to make positive contributions when reasonable, and avoid harmful consequences to others, the organization will follow a form of the golden rule. When one considers their organization's place as corporate citizens in the community at large, this concern for the well being of others creates a long-term positive financial outlook and a winning result for all of society.

Marketing Industry Ethical Issues

A 2002 Duffey Communications and Roper ASW survey of adults in the United States points to specific issues regarding marketing practices. The respondents were asked to list advertising practices that they think dominate the industry. The resultant ranking of the ten most widely prevalent practices in advertising, along with the top two least observed practices as listed in Exhibit 1-1, demonstrates why a discussion about the ethics of these practices needs to be held. (Ad Narcissicism, Ad Nauseum, 2002)

Exhibit 1-1

Consumers' Ranking of the 10 Most Widely Prevalent Advertising Practices

1	Unrealistic standards of beauty
2	Exploiting children by convincing them to buy things that are bad or unnecessary
3	Being creative or entertaining with advertising
4	Reducing amount of product and charging the same price
5	Targeting specific groups and convincing them to buy things that are bad or unnecessary
6	Misleading/exaggerated health benefits
7	Misleading/exaggerated environmental benefits
8	Subliminal advertising
9	Makin unfair/misleading comparisons
10	Using online services to provide more detailed information

Consumer's 2 Least Observed Advertising Practices

1	Using advertising to teach good values to young people
2	Incorporating and promoting positive role models

Source: Marketing News

With consideration of using chapter one's overview of marketing ethics, specific issues in the consumer behavior field will be examined in subsequent chapters. These issues have been selected because they cut across most industries and involve marketing techniques that are widely practiced by virtually all people in the marketing profession.

As the issues are explored, one must always keep in mind that as with any ethical issues, at times possibilities may exist that suggest means to address these concerns while at other times the profession itself is unsure how to best proceed. Chapter 2 examines the use of fear appeals in advertising. Do marketers have the right to scare consumers into purchasing their products? Chapter 3 discusses the nature of intrusive advertising. In the crowded media market, companies experience more and more difficulty trying to catch consumers' attention. How far should marketers be allowed to enter a consumer's life? Chapter 4 takes a look at the world of child marketing. Where, when, and how much should companies market to children? Should all marketing take into consideration the age of the target market? Chapter 5 studies the ramifications of the American consumer materialistic culture and how much responsibility companies should take for the materialistic values held by consumers in the United States. Chapter 6 explores the impact of super-thin, or waif female models on women's health habits and on the recent developments of the Adonis male image that affect men's health choices. Chapter 7 looks at the use of puffery, or exaggerated claims about a company's products. Should companies be allowed to puff and when does puffing move into deceptive advertising? A hot topic in the marketing field is

9

gathering consumer information in order to provide more personalized service. However, many organizations seek out as many revenue streams as possible and sell customers' private information, often without the consumers realizing what is happening. Chapter 8 looks at the ethics of gathering, safeguarding, and using consumer data. Chapter 9 sums up the key ethical issues presented in the preceding chapters while attempting to make sensible recommendations in light of ethical considerations discussed in chapter 1.

While each of these ethical marketing issues are discussed separately, the reader will most likely find that many aspects of the ethical subjects under discussion intertwined in a variety of ways. For example, the next chapter which debates the relative effectiveness of scare tactics in advertising must also address the relative merits regarding the use of fear appeals on adults versus children as well as the implications of marketing's influence on the American materialist life style. Some issues represent interesting conundrums while others present themselves with opportunities if Americans have the wherewithal to pursue alternatives that could make the problems more manageable. Corporations spend more time, energy, and money than any other sector of society to persuade individuals how to spend their time and money. They now need to examine the ethical ramifications of the results of their expenditures.

Chapter 2

"We Mean No Harm!" – The Use of Fear Appeals

"Fear is the prison of the heart."
-   *Anonymous*

What is a Fear Appeal?

In a famous 1980's ad, viewers saw an image of an egg being broken into a frying pan while an announcer asserted "This is your brain. This is your brain on drugs. Any questions?" The intent of the commercial's sponsor was to scare potential users from trying drugs. Another anti-drug ad aired by the Wyoming Department of Health at the time of this writing shows a man lifting a human brain out of a container and placing it on a meat slicer. As wet slices of brain land on top of each other, the announcer asks viewers how much brain they are willing to lose to meth. (Frazer, 2006)

Hyman and Tansey define a fear appeal as "An ad that arouses fear in the viewer regarding the effect of the viewer's suboptimal life style." (Hyman & Tansey, 1990) An effective fear appeal creates consumer stress and anxiety as a response to a threat that expresses or implies some form of danger. Fear appeals are generally regarded as a means to startle and frighten the ad's intended audience by describing the terrible results that will happen to them if they do not follow the actions that the marketer recommends. As a persuasive tactic, fear appeals often involve a threat to a person's self-concept. A fear appeal often implies that something is wrong with the way one thinks or acts so they need to change. By suggesting that one needs to change further implies an inadequacy in the consumer. Marketers use fears to garner consumer attention to their marketing communication and to generate interest in products designed to reduce those fears. Exhibit 2-1 demonstrates the intent of a fear appeal ad

Exhibit 2-1
The Intent to Fear Appeals

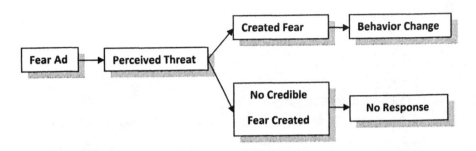

The marketer's goal is to employ fear to change consumer attitudes, intentions, and ultimately behavior. For this change to be effective, a fear appeal must:

1. Scare the target audience.
2. Offer a specific suggestion for overcoming the fear or threat.
3. The recommended action must be perceived by the target market as effective for reducing that threat.
4. The message recipient believes that he or she can perform the recommended action.

Commonly advertised fears address consumers' physical, safety, social, and self-esteem needs. An analysis of a weekday evening prime time network television programming revealed that over 60% of aired ads used fear appeals.[1] The observed ads that evening were represented by 18 physical, 16 safety, 16 social, and 8 esteem fear appeals. Many physical fear appeals attempted to show

---

[1] A total of 96 ads were aired of which 58 contained an element of fear. The programming included a mixture of comedy and dramatic shows.

how a particular drug could alleviate a health condition such as allergies. Car and truck manufacturers appealed to consumer safety concerns by demonstrating the safety of their vehicles. Cellular phone service providers often showed the impacts on family and friends when the competitors phone service didn't prove to be effective. Many beauty products preyed on woman's self-esteem anxieties, such as the fear of showing one's age. In all cases the marketers appeared to follow all the steps to create a successful fear appeal listed in the previous paragraph.

The Ethical Issues

Marketers typically use scare tactics through two approaches: fear of a negative consequence for not using the product and fear of a negative outcome associated with a certain behavior. One often employed scare tactic is for the marketer to suggest an unfavorable outcome if the consumer chooses the competitor's product. For example, a recently aired television ad suggested their body lotion was the only one that "tingles on contact" – suggesting that if the consumer used another brand of lotion they were using an inferior product. A weed killer that works in the rain raises the fear that use of a competitor's product may prove ineffective because rain will wash away the weed killer.

Raising consumer anxieties through fear appeals raises specific ethical issues. Some experts view this form of emotional marketing to represent a fair approach to helping the intended target market to avoid irresponsible behavior or to help consumers with solutions to an individual or societal problem. Others say that scare tactics can be controversial because they unfairly play on people's emotions and cause them to unnecessarily purchase products to resolve a problem made up by the marketer. At times, marketers have been accused of propagating a problem in order to create unnecessary fears that might not have existed before. Advertisers may also be tempted to over exaggerate the scare tactic in ways that exploit people's emotions. The threat in a fear appeal may appear more coercive than persuasive in nature. Marketing scare tactics may appear unethical if the

13

advertised solution does not eliminate or reduce the consumer's anxiety produced by the fear. The act of inspiring fear may be perceived as harmful by its very nature and intrusiveness making it unacceptable by societal standards of common decency. (Arthur & Queste, 2003)

The Effectiveness of Fear Appeals

Do scare tactics work? If so, why do they work, and when, if ever, can a marketer use them in an ethical way? In order to discuss the effect of fear appeals on consumers' behavior, an understanding how consumers form an attitude, or evaluation of their object under decision must first be explored. Expectancy-value models explain how consumers form and change attitudes based on their beliefs they have about an object or action and their evaluation of these particular beliefs. One expectancy-value model, the theory of reasoned action, provides an explanation of how, when, and why attitudes predict consumer behavior. The model, outlined in Exhibit 2-2, suggests that consumer beliefs and their consequent evaluation about an act, along with normative influences guide consumers to form an attitude toward the act which in turn influences the consumer's behavioral intention. Furthermore, the more specific the attitude is to the behavior of interest, the more likely the attitude will be related to the behavior. (Hoyer & MacInnis, 2004)

From Exhibit 2-1, fear appeals typically present a threat that may elevate anxieties in a consumer. According to the theory of reasoned action, the consumer may then examine their beliefs as to whether the threat is credible and evaluate if the marketer's suggested solution will resolve the threat. A consumer may take into account normative influences and then form an attitude which may lead to the behavioral intention and ultimately lead to the desired consumer behavior of purchasing the product or engaging in the behavior that eases the fear.

The theory of reasoned action suggests four strategies to change consumer attitudes and intentions:

1. Change consumer beliefs. One watch manufacturer implies that if you don't use their watch you may be missing the latest technological innovations. Their tagline: "More than a watch."
2. Change consumer evaluations. A synthetic oil outlines why their product protects your engine better than ordinary oil so your engine can "fight the enemy within."
3. Add a new belief to the consumer's belief set. One cosmetic company advertises "Three signs of tired skin. Gone! In One smooth move."
4. Target normative beliefs. A car manufacturer asks "Do 30 million people know something you don't know?"

Exhibit 2-2

The Theory of Reasoned Action

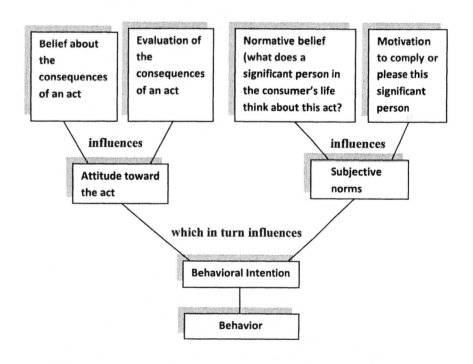

Researchers have sought to describe a direct relationship between fear and attitude change. Irving Janis from the Department of Psychology at Yale University arrived at an examination of fear levels and their resultant effect on behavior. He arrived at an "inverted U" as described in Exhibit 2-3. Irving demonstrated how low and high levels of fear arousal tend to be less effective on influencing people's attitude than moderate fear arousals. (Janis, 1967) In conjunction with the theory of reasoned action, the "Inverted U" model suggests that a minor threat will not garner a consumers' attention or not scare them enough to consider an evaluation of their attitudes to create a behavioral change such as purchasing a product that would alleviate that threat. On the other hand, too grave a threat may appear too high handed or simply not credible. In that case the consumer may simply ignore the threat.

Exhibit 2-3

Fear Appeals: The 'Inverted U' Hypothesis

Attitude change

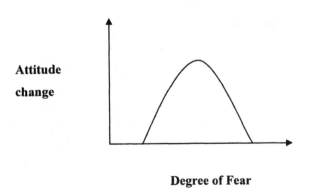

Degree of Fear

How do marketers avoid the cynical implications that they use fear to unnecessarily create anxieties in consumers? Unethical fear appeals can backfire and damage the image of the advertiser if careful consideration of the scare tactic is not considered. Marketers should carefully consider the threat used to generate the fear when designing their advertising, as it may prove to be difficult to

16

identify which specific factors a consumer will consider when making an ethical judgment. Marketers need to keep in mind that the fear appeal ethically persuades a consumer rather than coerce them into a poor decision that does not benefit them. Marketers should consider pre-testing ads that employ fear appeals before introducing an advertising campaign aimed at changing consumer behavior. (Arthur & Queste, 2003) Finally, a business must always act with integrity. The higher the credibility of the company, the more likely those consumers will consider the fear appeal to be credible.

Chapter 3

"Pardon the Interruption" - Intrusive Advertising in Consumers' Daily Lives

"We're drowning in images. The moving image boards (MIBs) have completely changed the landscape of America and, slowly the rest of the world. The MIB's are pollution, pure and simple – image pollution. When I say pollution, I'm referring to the manner in which they have defiled and corrupted our lives. In fact, I do believe that MIBs defile us spiritually. They crowd out reality, batter us with constant commerce."

- *Kurt Wenzel*

The Future of Advertising

Author Kurt Wenzel and movie director Steven Spielberg provide visions of what the future of advertising might look like. They include subplots in their book and movie that demonstrate the extent to which marketers may intrude on our lives. In his book, "Exposure," Wenzel sees billboards evolving into Moving Image Boards consisting of digital plasma screens, some of which are hundreds of feet high, some on the sides of buildings, other smaller ones on public bathroom mirrors or in bathroom stalls, all constantly pitching ads at people. At one point, even smaller MIBs are sold to individuals that were strapped on their bodies; a human billboard if you will. To escape all the pressures of this intrusive marketing, one of Wenzel's characters even pays $20,000 a week to attend "Camp Silencio," a barebones retreat where "no pods, money, credit cards, and sound or anxiety-making devices of any kinds" are allowed. Visitors to the camp are warned to "refrain from humming advertising jingles or discussion of media of any sort with residents." Camp attendees spend their days in various meditation exercises to rid their minds of marketing clutter that polluted their brains.

In the film Minority Report, Steven Spielberg looks at life in the United States fifty years from now. Spielberg depicts the use of widely placed retina scanners that constantly identify and track people in order to identify their wants and needs. This encroachment technology allows companies to track what people buy so they know what they need and can keep pitching personal sales messages. In a particularly interesting scene, the main protagonist, John Anderton (played by Tom Cruise), walks down a sidewalk while scanners read the retinas of his eyes. He is bombarded with personalized advertising messages from three dimensional billboards. (Spielberg, 2002)

Do these seem like science fiction? Consider the following day in the life of a business professional. He or she rises out of bed and turns on the morning news show on television to check on the weather and road traffic for the morning commute. The morning news show is continuously interrupted by commercials and by promotions of that evening's shows. He goes out to get the paper, noticing an advertisement for a lawyer in the form of a post-it note stuck on top of the paper. The paper itself is in a plastic bag containing further advertising that includes a sample. The newspaper contains 50% advertising content and also several sales circulars that fall out while he tries to unfold the paper to read it. He decides to enjoy some cereal for his breakfast. The cereal box features a special promotion for a new movie that has just been released. As he gets dressed he notices brand labels on his new pants. As he rides to work he passes numerous billboards that clutter the roadways. He listens to the local radio morning show that also airs many ads. As the businessman travels to work he decides to stop at his local convenience store to pick up a cup of coffee. All manners of ads – from lotteries to in-store specials - bombard him. When he arrives at work, the businessman turns on his computer. He notices his email box is jammed with spam. When he checks out web sites (for business purposes of course!) ads start

20

popping up on the computer screen. He even finds the web sites contain a great deal of advertising on them. By noon, hungry and stressed from work, he decides to head out with some colleagues to grab a bite for lunch. He notices ads everywhere – on buildings, on the sides of busses, and even at the ATM, where he stops to obtain some cash to buy lunch. When he stops at the restaurant's restroom, he finds himself staring at an ad above the urinal. On the evening drive home, he realizes he needs to run some errands. He stops to fuel up his car and is faced with ads on and around the gas pumps. He stops at the supermarket to pick up some items for dinner that evening. The supermarket's PA system blares out promotions and he notices ads on the walls, floors, and even on many products themselves. Upon arriving home, he checks his voice mail to find several ad pitches. He sorts through his mail, 90% of which are ads, or junk mail. His children are at home completing their homework including a corporate sponsored reading contest. After dinner he decides to relax and watch a little television only to find commercial breaks, product placements in shows, and network promotions popping up on screen in the middle of the show he's watching. Tired of this he decides to switch over to watch his favorite baseball team play. The game features TV time outs for commercial breaks, ads along the stadium, digitally inserted ads placed by the broadcast channel, and continuous sponsored promotions. Having had enough for one day, he decides to call it a night and goes to bed with the anticipation of facing a similar day tomorrow morning![2]

The Elements of Intrusive Advertising

Advertising messages that arrive uninvited especially in a non-shopping environment constitute intrusive advertising. Any of the following criteria in particular qualify an ad as intrusive:

1. You can't turn it off.
2. The ad enters your private space without permission.
3. You're a captive audience.

---

[2] Based on author's actual experience.

4. The ad doesn't support anything, or it costs you money.

Oddly, in a time when consumers have more access to information than ever, they also find themselves overwhelmed. The process of commercialization has permeated American culture. As illustrated in the previous section, Americans now face a commercial clutter of 3,000 to 5,000 marketing communications daily. Desensitized consumers somehow cope with this barrage of information through avoidance and screening techniques. As our environment becomes overloaded with sales pitches, companies find they experience a harder time reaching consumers. So much ad content exists in most media that consumers have learned to deal only with the content they want. In what unfortunately often becomes the easiest approach to dealing with this issue, marketers work to create more advertising through sensory triggers that are louder, splashier, and even more intrusive in their attempt to garner consumers' attention.

In some ways the advertising industry has been built on intruding on people's lives. Exhibit 3-1 illustrates the communications model that most companies apply in their marketing strategies. The marketer generates and encodes a marketing message that is sent through a communications channel and then hopefully decoded by the consumer recipient. Ideally, the consumer will provide feedback to the company as to the impact of the message. At any point along the communications flow, consumers may experience noise, or any interference that keeps the marketing communication from being received fully by the consumer. This noise could come from simply not paying attention, divided attention, or simply too much activity in people's lives that prevents them from taking in the marketing message. For example, too many intrusive, interruptive advertisements from too many sources create too much competition for people's attention – in essence, too much noise that interferes with the reception of the message.

The traditional advertising model typically supports content aimed at consumers. Radio and television programs are in effect sponsored by the advertisers. If a consumer wishes to watch or listen to a show, he or she expects that the program will be periodically interrupted by periodically by ads. When a person reads a magazine or a newspaper, they understand that the accompanying advertising helps to reduce the cost of the publication to the consumer. The problem for marketers is that as consumers encounter more ad clutter, the marketing message has a harder time to catch a consumer's attention. This is all occurring at a time when people take on more activities that create time pressures in their lives, another form of noise that leaves consumers less attentive to the ads pitched to them.

To combat the competition for consumers' attention, companies are resorting to tactics that differ from traditional marketing. More money is now spent on unusual or intrusive ways to try to break through all the noise. For instance, many companies are constantly trying to change ad campaigns in order to try to capture consumer attention with new and fresh messages. Another technique is to design ads to be more creative and unusual hoping that the new approach will garner the consumers' attention. Along a similar vein, companies are creating ads that are more and more controversial. The issue with all these approaches is that they tend to increase a company's advertising expense while adding to the advertising clutter (creating more noise) and even more competition for consumers' attention.

According to Seth Godin, Vice-President of Direct Marketing for Yahoo!, traditional marketing has resulted in the following paradigms:

1. People have a finite amount of attention.
2. People have a finite amount of money.
3. The more products offered the less there is to go around.
4. In order to capture more attention and more money, traditional marketers must increase spending.

5. To increase marketing exposure, companies must be willing to increase their advertising expenditures substantially.
6. Spending more on advertising simply adds to the advertising clutter which means the more companies spend, the less their advertising works.

The result is that as the marketplace becomes more cluttered, companies resort to intrusive advertising to break through all the noise. (Godin, 1999)

Exhibit 3-1

The Communications Model

Noise

| Encodes | Communication | Decoded by |
| Message | Channel | Receiver |

Communicator

Feedback

Intrusive Marketing Practices

How do marketers try to intrude into consumer lives and why don't these techniques work? One marketing strategy that companies have been exploiting extensively in order to avoid much of the noise comes through the use of product placement. Products are embedded in television shows, movies, sporting venues, and any other media that marketers think might serve as a means to garner attention. Movies and sporting events in particular represent a captive audience where people have no choice but to be exposed to the product commercialization. Advertisers look for a closed environment while producers and investors look for extra sources of revenues.

Movie studios and producers have a particularly long history of product placement. DeBeers paid for placement of diamonds in movies in the 1950's. Gordon's Gin paid to have Katherine Hepburn's character toss their product overboard in The African Queen. In 1971 the sales of magnum 44 guns went through the roof after Dirty Harry was released. Reeses Pieces also experienced an incredible increase in sales after Steven Spielberg's E.T. was released in 1982. The rush was on to place products in movies from that point on. Huggies paid $100,000 to place their product in 1987's Baby Boom, Exxon $300,000 to appear on Tom Cruise's Days of Thunder, and Lark cigarettes doled out $350,000 to be James Bond smoke in License to Kill. In addition, most movie studios are part of a conglomerate so that the productions themselves are constantly promoted in other media owned by the conglomerate. One good example of a company who effectively use cross promoting is Disney who own ABC and ESPN. So the advertising glut becomes circular – a Disney movie that includes product placements advertised on its own stations. The movie typically has cross merchandising as well with many of their movie characters appearing on DVD's, clothes, and toys, as well as in soundtracks, theme parks and so forth. (Behind the Scenes: Hollywood Goes Hypercommercial, 2000)

Product placement is typically arranged through one of three means:

25

- It simply happens as a normal part of the script and no compensation to the product's producer is involved.
- It's arranged with some form of non-financial compensation involved. For example, by agreeing to supply the product to the production, the company will gain audience exposure.
- It's arranged with financial compensation to the studio.

Product placement takes place at three levels: in the background, in dialog, or with the star using and enjoying the product. Judges on American Idol drink Coca-Cola while the host tells fans they can submit their votes on AT&T wireless. (Neer) Companies that use product placement in movies do so primarily because they have a captive audience. On television product placement tries to circumvent those audience members who either simply switch channels when commercials come on or zip through a show they've recorded. Evidently product placement on television has proven to be an effective strategy as the number of placements grew by 30% from 2004 to 2005. Marketers shelled out $941 million to integrate brands into television shows in 2005. (More Ad Pitches Could Get Embedded, 2006)

Advertising Age listed product placement as the number one ad issue to watch in 2006. Consumer Watch, a buyer protection agency, has petitioned both the FTC and the FCC to try to get the television industry to stop the practice. One FCC commissioner said that undisclosed product placement could be payola and illegal – especially in shows that look like news. (Wood, 2005) The payola refers to the illegal practice of paying studios to place a product without viewers knowing that payment has been made. Another ethical product placement concern is if the product is used in a way that is deceptive to the viewer. A car that escapes unscathed after a wild chase may make the car seem capable of withstanding terrific abuse that simply wouldn't hold up in the real world. Defenders of product placement suggest that all they are doing is reflecting the real world, that products can add a sense of realism to a movie or television show.

They also add that they believe the average viewer doesn't care about product placement issues. (Edwards, 2006)

Product placements are spreading to other media and consumer products. Consider the following intrusions on a captive audience. A marketing firm threw parties for a company that manages dorm style apartments near college campuses. When prospective student tenants checked out the apartments, they found them filled with name brand furniture and cosmetics. The company's president believes students are more open to product placement marketing because they are extremely brand conscious and tend to be early adopters. (Chafkin, 2006) Advertisers spent $56 million in 2005 to place advertising in videogames. One report suggests that at least 132 million gamers thirteen years and older playing in the United States. One reason for the recent explosion in game advertising is the move from static to dynamic ads. For example, one video game that features a car chase contains a name brand car on a billboard. The billboard changes, demonstrating different features on the advertised car each time the player plays this particular videogame. (Ramirez, 2006)

Various studies report that a half-second exposure to an in-game ad suffices for a player to notice it and that 75% of players engage with at least one ad per minute. The videogame product placement industry is forecasted to grow to a $1 billion dollar market by 2010. (Enright, 2007) In a similar vein, companies are targeting comic books for product placements. General Motors, Nike, and Daimler-Chrysler have all recently worked with comics publishers to place their brands and emblems in comics as a way to reach young adult males. (Steinberg, 2006) ATM's have proven an effective means to pitch products to people. As a consumer makes a withdrawal, they typically wait for the transaction to process. Many advertisers view this time and the fact that consumers are getting cash in hand as the perfect opportunity to market a spending opportunity on their products. Screens now play ads, jingles, and may even dispense coupons with the consumer's bank statement. Convenience stores now feature LED displays, ads on the nozzles, and broadcasts at their gas pumps.

27

The number of flat screens with wireless marketing transmissions in elevators has proliferated. One marketing company that features elevator marketing goes by the interesting name Captivate. (Is Any Place Sacred? Nah.) In New York City some taxis now come equipped with a video monitor that has no mute button. (Moore, 2003) Many municipalities today are trying to increase their revenues on selling ad space on metro busses, subways, and even on police cars. One company, Government Acquisitions LLC, pitches advertising to towns and cities as a means to supplement their budgets. Under a contractual agreement, the company provides patrol cars (complete with advertising) for three years. The company retains all the advertising revenue. (This Bust's for You: Police Are Considering Selling Ad Space on Their Patrol Cars, 2002) Sometimes governments can get too carried away looking for more revenues. Florida motorists sued Imagitas, a subsidiary of Pitney Bowes, because the company placed advertising inside automobile registration packets mailed to Florida car owners. (Word, 2006) An energy supplier supported a city's park and lake improvement and was recognized with a sign on the site recognizing their $1.5 million financial contribution but also featured the company's brand logo. The city mayor justified the sign by stating that it was no different than a construction sign. Other civic leaders stated that the sign was not advertising but rather recognition of a company's contribution to the community. However, other citizens have contacted the city office to express their concerns and the fact that they weren't notified in advance. (Schumacher, 2007)

Intrusive ads drive internet and cell phone users crazy. Anyone who surfs the web regularly copes with all manners of pop-up advertising. Because advertising hasn't effectively served as a source of revenues for web sites, web sites and advertisers try to work harder to gather our attention by delivering bigger, splashier promotions. Consumers resent these intrusions on their web surfing as Exhibit 3-2 demonstrates.

Companies advertising with pop-ups may actually see their reputations degraded. One survey of internet users found that more than 50% of the respondents reported that pop-up ads affect their opinion of the advertiser very negatively and nearly 40% reported that pop-ups affected their opinion of the web site very negatively. One consumer reaction is to defend themselves against pop-ups by obtaining ad-blocking software. Despite all the adverse reaction to this form of marketing web advertisers continually risk annoying a large audience with the hope of reaching a few interested customers, spending an estimated $1.5 billion in 2006. (Nielsen, 2004)

Another form of intrusive internet marketing that drives consumers crazy is the use of spam, or unsolicited mass emails. One of the main reasons mass emails persist is that inexpensive lists along with inexpensive technology makes this approach a cheap form of marketing. Unfortunately, well-intentioned internet retailers often take a poor approach to managing their email marketing tactics. One survey of internet users revealed that more than 70% of the respondents believe it is somewhat likely that spammers targeted them because they had shopped online. This lack of trust hurts those legitimate companies that do business online. Some additional issues with spam will be discussed in the chapter that deals with privacy issues. (Spam, Spam, Spam, Spam)

One last relatively new intrusive marketing method is the practice of stealth marketing. One company hired actors to demonstrate a product without the consumer realizing they're being marketed to. Two actors, posing as a couple, for instance, roam Times Square in New York City asking passersby to take their picture for them with the couple's new cell phone and digital camera attachment. Two other young female actresses stopped at a bar on Manhattan's East Side, got a drink at the bar and started discussing their new cell phone. In just a minute, they were surrounded by men who were curious to learn more. Another young actor enters a coffee shop where he pulls out a laptop computer and plays a new game. Soon others are checking out the game. Gary Ruskin, Executive Director of Commercial Alert, states that this form of marketing is deceptive because the consumers targeted don't know that they are speaking with actors pitching a product. The companies involved claim that their actors will identify themselves if asked. Most companies report positive feedback and that this technique was an innovative way to sell a product. (Beattie, 2002)

Exhibit 3-2

Consumer Reactions to Pop-up Advertising

Design Element	Users Answering "Very Negatively" or "Negatively"
Pops-up in front of your window	95%
Loads slowly	94%
Tries to trick you into clicking on it	94%
Does not have a "close" button	93%
Covers what you are trying to see	93%
Doesn't say what it is for	92%
Moves content around	92%
Occupies most of the page	90%
Blinks on and off	87%
Floats across the screen	79%
Automatically plays sound	79%

Source: Jakob Nielsen's Alertbox

Companies use another form of stealth marketing by hiring companies to check out and enter chat rooms, discussion groups, and newsgroups that contain potential customers. The hired guns often represent themselves as a satisfied customer. If no one online responds to them, then they will form aliases and double or triple keyboard and hope to create an online buzz. One example of companies who successfully manage this technique is record producers who hire people to chat on line about a new recording coming out on the market. (Fan - or Phony?)

Another area of intrusive advertising worth noting is at sport events. Whether one watches the game on television, online, or in person, you can be certain of being bombarded by numerous ads. NASCAR drivers and their cars serve as a classic example of product placement in a sports event. The drivers and their cars are plastered with their sponsor's logos, in effect serving as billboards for their sport. Even NASCAR's racing series, the Nextel Cup, is sponsored. Pro Golfing Association's golfers are just a little more subtle, but wear clothing lines with brand names and most wear a hat that features the brand name of the golf equipment line they use. Their golf balls are often visible. The names of pro golf tournaments over the years have evolved from celebrity sponsors to corporate sponsors. Jockeys in the Kentucky Derby wear sponsors' patches. National Hockey League features advertising on the dasherboards and even in the ice itself. Team sports tend to use their stadiums and broadcasts as their marketing tools. (Rovell, 2004) Most sports stadiums now feature corporate sponsored names. One team plans to start their games at 7:11 p.m. because of a $1.5 million three year deal with 7-Eleven.

A 2007 regular season major league baseball game four hour radio broadcast featured a total of 124 marketing messages consisting of commercials and sponsorships including 30 marketing pitches in a radio pregame, 71 marketing communications in the game itself, and another 22 in the post-game radio broadcast. The same game as televised featured a remarkable 475 marketing exposures including commercials, sponsors, and advertising exposure of in stadium banners and signs. Dugouts featured advertising and Gatorade product placement. A banner was digitally inserted behind home plate and was changed every half inning. The count of marketing exposures did not include partial glimpses of signs and the number of times the camera angle reshot back to the batter. Also not included are the names of the teams and the player uniforms, both of which Major League Baseball actively market. Including those

31

possibilities the number of marketing pitches most likely exceeded 1,000 exposures.[2]   Major League baseball is also looking at possible marketing opportunities by advertising on the on-deck circles, the bases, and even possibly the uniforms themselves. (Rovell, 2004) Rick Reilly, a feature writer for Sports Illustrated wrote a humorous column on the direction sports marketing may be headed, which included the following observation using Al Michaels, a football announcer describing a run for a touchdown:

> "He's across the fifty! Past the Colt 45! What a move at the Century 21!
> To the 9 Lives line! The Motel 6! The One-der Bread! Do you believe in
> Miracle Whip? Yes!"

Intrusive forms of advertising have even invaded where we shop. Shoppers now face floors that talk, messages that swoop down from the ceiling, motion sensors that trigger on-shelf light shows, and floor signs. Floorgraphics creates both decals that adhere to the floor and talking floor ads, where an audio commercial is triggered when customers step on a designated spot.   Island Display created Skybox which shines brand messages into backlit billboards for point of purchase promotions.   Crew Design created Visi-strobe, a motion activated device that triggers individual items to light up and highlight particular products when a shopper walks by. One new wireless hand held high tech device allows consumers to scan products while they shop. The device can interact with the internet and can let shoppers know when photos, deli items, or prescriptions are ready while they browse through the store. All these items try to garner consumer attention and to cut through the noise in the customers' shopping experience. Ironically, they also add to the noise that shoppers experience at the same time. (Fitzgerald, 2004)

---

[2] Cleveland Indians VS. Minnesota Twins, September 5, 2007.

Intrusive Advertising V.S. Permission Marketing

Marketers create much of the noise that consumers deal with through their screening. How can marketers break through this clutter overload and reach consumers? Reviewing the criteria that describes what makes an ad intrusive provides suggestions on how marketers can improve. The first two criteria in particular describe the need to ask consumers for their permission to market to them, personalize, and provide consumers with control over the marketing itself. But this process requires patience and trust. A company must demonstrate they are acting in the consumer's best interest by acting with full integrity at all times.

The result, Seth Godin believes, is marketing that consumers anticipate, is personal, and is relevant. People look forward, rather than dreading, to hearing personalized, interesting, and relevant messages from the company. (Godin, 1999) Marketers need to collect information on what customers buy, why they buy, what they browse and don't buy, and which offers have converted them in the past. On line, marketers need to design ads that indicate what will happen if people click on them, clearly identify their ads, and present information about what is being advertised; in other words, speak plainly, make the options clear, and provide the information that consumers want. (Nielsen, 2004) Once a relationship is established, providing a customized, interactive experience will be appreciated by consumers. Customization empowers consumers while giving them a sense of individual identity with the company. Interactivism creates emotional branding and an affinity between consumer and company. (Counts, 2006)

People don't necessarily dislike advertising. Consumers object to intrusive, controlling advertising. A study on marketing resistance by consumers showed record levels of consumer resistance to marketing efforts. Consumers cited the level of saturation and intrusiveness as the one particularly marketing practice they disliked. Consumers desire marketing that engages them in a more satisfying way. They want marketing that shows more respect for their time and attention. (2005 Marketing Receptivity Survey, 2005)

33

Seeking permission, personalizing, and granting consumers' control over marketing requires more work and time, but the investment is rewarding. Jack Tar American Tavern uses email to boost visibility. The restaurant sends e-mail newsletters to its loyalty members who elect to sign up for the service. E-mails are individualized and targeted based on the client's order history and location. (Dilworth, 2006) Chevy Chase Supermarket, an upscale Washington metro grocery store uses mobile phone marketing to alert their customers of specials. Customers sign up for the program in the store or on the company's web site. When a shipment of fresh blueberries arrived at the store, they alerted customers enrolled in the program. Customers could interactively communicate with the store by texting back messages such as "Hold 2 baskets for me." The average purchase by regular customers is $30.53 while those enrolled in the program spend an average of $58.79. (Dilworth D. , 2006) Benchmark Auto Group of Huntsville, Alabama decided to work on ongoing customer relationships with an electronic newsletter. The company had a data base of names that were warehoused and almost forgotten about. So they created an individualized email with lifestyle articles, vehicle reviews, and promotions. The typical email open rate is 2%; nearly two out of three recipients of Benchmark's newsletter open it. (Fielding, 2006) A 2006 Forrester Research Survey reinforces this perspective by demonstrating that consumers' highest level of trust regarding an advertising source was with e-mail they had signed up for. (Research, 2007) The Direct Marketing Association reports that the prices of business to consumer permission-based email had the largest price drop of all email marketing in 2006. (Abramovich, 2007) Conversely, Exhibit 3-3 demonstrates how these permission based emails had the highest opening rates.

In his book Permission Marketing, Seth Godin describes building a relationship like dating. So instead of asking everyone in sight to go out on a date with your company, consider ways to instead get to know the person and build up a trusting relationship where both parties enter into a win-win situation.

Exhibit 3-3

Permission Email Open Rates

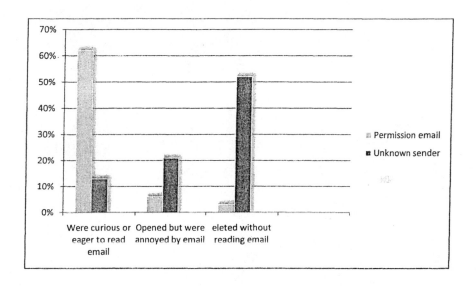

Source: Marketing News January 6, 2003

Chapter 4

Are Marketers Robbing Kids of Their Childhood?

"When it comes to the care and protection and well-being of children, our world's most precious resource, there is a special responsibility to provide them with products and programs that are at least neutral in any good or bad impact they might have on them, and at best products that are positive in their impact. At the same time it is our responsibility to protect the world's children from products and programs that can be shown to have significant deleterious impact. The greatest danger is not overt evil intent, but the failure of child-targeted product and program creators, developers, marketers, and decision makers to stand up and act on what they know to be true regarding products and programs with potential to damage children's bodies or minds."

- Dan Acuff

A Historical Perspective

To marketers, children represent an important target because they embody three different markets. First children directly spend money. Children also influence a great deal of family spending. Possibly the most important market for organizations to consider is the future market. Companies recognize that consumer habits and brand loyalties are often formed when children are young and can be carried through to adulthood.

This topic arguably represents the most controversial ethical matter in the marketing profession today. The size and economic impact of the children's market is staggering. Consider the following statistics regarding this market also often referred to as "Generation Y" or "Millennials:

- The number of children under 18 in the United States has grown from 47.3 million in 1950 to 73.5 million in 2005. (U.S. Population Estimtes by Age, Sex, Race, and Hispanic Origin , 2005)

37

- This age group now comprises 25% of the U.S. population. (U.S. Population Estimtes by Age, Sex, Race, and Hispanic Origin , 2005)
- Children between the ages of eight and fourteen spent an average $1,294 in 2004. As a group they spent a total of $38 billion. (Kennedy, 2004)
- Children ages four to twelve influence over $670 billion of parental decisions ranging from small grocery items to the family car. (Kelly & Kulman, 2004)
- Businesses spent over an estimated $1 billion in advertising to this market segment in 2004. (Whitney, 2005)
- Two-thirds of children aged 8 to 18 have televisions in their bedrooms and two thirds live in homes with cable TV. (Brody, 2005)
- Children aged 2 to 17 on average watched 15,000 to 18,000 hours of television and viewed an estimated 40,000 commercials annually compared with 12,000 hour spent per year at school. (Bagdikian, 2000)
- Children aged 8 to 18 years old are exposed to more than 8 1/2 hours of media messages per day. (Roberts, Foehr, & Rideout, June)

These statistics point out why so many businesses seek out this potentially lucrative market and why many organizations may be tempted to pursue questionable means to gain children's business. The hard reality is that companies with the money and resources that can be brought to bear on this market are often the ones that make the most money.

To understand the present state of the children's market, examining the history of marketing to this demographic segment provides some helpful insights regarding the give and take of stakeholders in this market. In the 1920's advertisers sought to create an alliance with mothers by convincing them that the product was beneficial for the child. The 1930's and 1940's saw the first pediatrician and child psychologists to endorse infant and toddler toys. (Thomas, 2007) Ads in the 1950's tended to be low budget in nature and focused on the attributes of the product. Pressure tactics and deceptive forms of advertising were commonplace. Selling techniques were unregulated, not having to distinguish between fantasy and reality. Schools were heavily targeted; one researcher found that 97 percent of teachers interviewed in a study used corporate sponsored materials. (Molnar, 1996) In the 1960's the three major television networks began to group most of their children's program offerings together on Saturday morning. This tactic generated much higher proportions of child viewers than had previously been obtained when children's content was aired at diverse times throughout the week. (Barnouw, 1970)

By 1974, the Federal Communications Commission (FCC) recognized that children were vulnerable to these forms of marketing and enacted regulations on the number and types of ads targeted to children. In 1978, the Federal Trade Commission (FTC) issued a report that children under age seven did not possess the cognitive ability to adequately evaluate child-oriented television – in essence unable to separate the difference between fact and fantasy. But with a change of administrations, the FTC backed off of its position and Congress took away its power to regulate children's advertising. The 1980's saw a marked increase in the number of women entering the work force. With mothers at work and latchkey children home alone, marketers had unfettered access to reach children while they were alone. In addition, companies turned to ethnographic methods by interviewing and observing children in their own homes. The goal was to examine children's private behaviors to gain marketing insights to more effectively reach that market segment. As a consequence, marketers started a fundamental shift from communicating to both parent and child and instead sought to separate the world of working parents and the newly evolved youth culture. Toy companies began to produce program length commercials with story

39

lines tied to product marketing. By 1987, 60 percent of all toys sold in the U.S. were based on license characters. Worrying about the invasiveness of marketers into children's lives, consumer activist groups sprung up in the 1990's to attempt to combat what they felt was unethical and manipulative influence over children. In 2004, the American Academy of Pediatrics advocated that inappropriate advertising contributes to many kids' ills, from obesity to anorexia, to drinking alcohol and having sex too soon and that regulation is needed. (Schor, 2004)

The Ethical Issues

With this historical background, a variety of ethical issues on child marketing emerges. An examination of some of the most controversial marketing practices reveals that many concerns regarding children is still evolving. Certainly, children represent the most defenseless segment of the population to engage in a media relationship. Children are just learning what to value, and marketing, for better or worse, can exert a powerful influence on the value formation of children. After reviewing these ethical matters, a look at possible solutions follows.

Young children tend to see advertising as simply entertaining and often part of the program they're watching. Although children can discriminate commercials from programs by the time they are five years old, a few more years are needed for children to understand advertising's persuasive intent. (Thomas G, Smith, Bengen, & Johnson, 1975) Research has demonstrated a definite impact of television advertising on children. One study measured children's recall of television advertisements. More than half of the children in the study tended to remember an ad for toys, cereals, and ice cream even when each ad is shown just once in a program. When children were asked where they learned about toys they desired, they most often identified television commercials as the source. Positive attitudes toward an advertised product typically persist over time, even though the ad has been forgotten. In another study, children have been shown to exhibit significant increases in desire for advertised merchandise. Another researcher found that the amount of television viewing was a significant predictor of children's purchase requests at the supermarket. Furthermore, the same researcher found that commercials offering premiums were more persuasive than commercials featuring popular cartoon characters. Television commercials targeted toward children appear highly effective at accomplishing their goal of increasing product sales. (Kunkel, Wilcox, Cantor, Palmer, Linn, & Dowrick, 2004)

Today marketers bypass parents and connect directly with the child, in effect isolating parents and at times joining forces with kids to influence parents on how to spend money. Marketers argue that children of the twenty-first century are far more sophisticated than previous generations. Increased responsibilities of children in homes because of working parents has led to a development called "Kids Are Getting Older Younger" (also know by its acronym KAGOY) and sometimes referred to as age compression. The concept of KAGOY suggests that children yearn to be older than they are. Today's grade school children play and act in ways that teens did in previous generations. (Thomas, 2007) One consequence of this tactic is to design products and craft marketing messages originally designed for older children and market them instead to grade school children. Action figures that were once targeted to boys aged eight to eleven are now marketed to boys as young as three. Teen magazines that once sold glamour to teens are now targeting eleven and twelve year old girls. Skimpy and revealing clothes are targeted to girls as young as four and five. A retailer came under fire for selling thong underwear with sexually suggestive phrases to seven to fourteen year olds. (Schor, 2004) Are children being robbed of their childhood or are marketers simply recognizing and reacting to a societal trend?

Another issue that arose from eliminating parents from marketing communications is the attempt to leverage children in many purchase decisions. Often referred to as pester power, marketers directly aim their marketing efforts at children to encourage them to ask and even nag their parents to purchase particular products. This tactic has proven particularly effective as the number of

41

single parent households has climbed and parents who work long hours often feel motivated by guilt to spend money on their kids. As Susan Linn, Associate Director of the Media Center at Judge Baker Children's Center in Boston, states "By encouraging children to nag, and by bombarding them with messages that material goods are the key to happiness, the marketing industry is taking advantage of parents' innate desire for their children to be happy." (Linn, 2004) One major retailer set up a holiday wish site featuring two elves who encourage kids to select toys by clicking on the word "yes" when a toy appears on the screen. Applause is played when "yes" is selected. But the site is silent if "no" is selected. Promises one elf, "If you show us what you want on your wish list, we'll send it straight off to your parents." (6 Strategies Marketers Use to Get Kids to Want Stuff Bad, 2006)   One researcher found that 70% of parents proved receptive to their children's product requests. Another industry expert found that items purchased for kids declined by one-third if kids did not ask for them. A current marketing practice is to advise clients that their products won't be purchased if they cannot get kids to request it. Is this tactic effective? A 2002 poll found that 83% of twelve to thirteen year old children reported that they have asked their parents to pay for or let them purchase an item the child had seen advertised. Forty percent did so for a product they thought their parents would disapprove. After parents denied a request, seventy-one percent of the children in the survey kept asking. The average number of requests is eight, but 25% of the kids asked more than ten times. Eleven percent asked more than fifty times. The result from all that nagging is an estimated $565 billion of purchases influenced by children aged four to twelve. (Rowe & Ruskin)

Interestingly, market research found that many mothers consult with kids and sometimes give them full control of a purchase. Many parents find, for example, that they save money by not purchasing items a child won't eat. (Schor, 2004) Exhibit 4-1 demonstrates how one researcher even categorized seven classes of nagging!   So, are marketers simply helping children make household decisions?

42

Exhibit 4-1

7 Nagging Tactics

Pleading	A nag accompanied by repletion of words such as "please" or "mom, mom, mom"
Persistent	A nag that involves constant requests for the desired product like "I'm gonna ask just one more time"
Forceful	Usually extremely pushy and may include subtle threats including "Well then, I'll just go ask Dad."
Demonstrative	Usually characterized by full-blown tantrums in public places
Sugar-coated	Promises affection in return for a purchase. May include a comment such as "You're the best Mom in the world!"
Threatening	Usually involves blackmail if an item isn't purchased. "If I can't get this I'll run away!"
Pity	The child claims he or she will be heartbroken, teased, or humiliated if parents refuse to buy a certain item.

Source: Kids as Customers: A Handbook of Marketing to Children by James McNeal

A technique used by companies to directly communicate to children is to reach them in a location once thought to represent a safe harbor from the outside world – our schools. Children spend approximately 40% of their weekdays in a classroom where traditional forms of advertising can't reach them. Companies were seeking ways to communicate to this captive audience. Meanwhile, school systems face funding pressures due to more demands at the same time that taxpayers wish to limit their tax burdens. As a consequence, school leaders look for alternative funding sources to help supplement constrained budgets. A Colorado Springs school district was one of the first to invite businesses to market in their schools. The school district was facing increasing enrollments and falling revenues. The leader of the district hired a professional to negotiate with corporate sponsors. One ten year exclusive distribution contract with a beverage supplier brought in $11 million to the district. The district also negotiated school bus, hallway, school newspaper, and stadium public address advertising. (Schlosser, 2002)

Businesses have been quite willing to step in with assistance as long as they gain marketing access to the student body. They argue that sponsored programs and advertising provide schools with desperately needed materials and support. Marketers suggest that students see commercials everywhere and there is no reason to believe that kids are unduly influenced by any additional advertising they see in school. Defenders of marketing in school also state that teachers are capable of evaluating materials for commercialism and to use the sponsored materials in an appropriate way, and even further that these sponsored materials serve as opportunities to teach media literacy.

In particular, marketing with an educational angle helps to provide product credibility to children and parents. Psychologists believe that the effect of in-school commercialism is stronger because students represent a captive audience and often required by teachers and school administrators to pat attention to advertising. Furthermore, research shows that expertise and prestige increase the power of a message's source; the prestige and expertise of school personnel may become associated with commercial items promoted on school grounds. (Kunkel, Wilcox, Cantor, Palmer, Linn, & Dowrick, 2004)

A case in point is Channel One Communications. In 1989, Channel One, a twelve minute free news and current events program that contains two minutes of commercials, began broadcasting directly into schools. Schools that signed a three year contract with the guarantee that 90 percent of their students would watch the program received video equipment as an incentive to carry the broadcast daily. The company made deals with 12,000 middle and secondary schools populated by forty percent of all American teens. The broadcast is reported to be only second to the Superbowl in audience size. Most importantly from Channel One's perspective is that the audience is captive with limited to no distractions. (Schor, 2004)

Other educational efforts by WRC, also known by previous generations by the name Weekly Reader, feature custom publishing offers with third party branded products. WRC's web site claims that "materials from third-party sources can be customized and targeted to an organization's specific business needs." (Sharing knowledge is essential in a thriving society, 2007) Pizza Hut has a well known program called "Book It," a program to reward reading in grades K-6. If the child meets the reading goal set by their classroom teacher, he or she will receive a Pizza Award Certificate for a free individual sized pizza. (About Book It, 2007) In 2004 the program was in 910,000 classrooms. While a worthy goal to encourage young readers, parents would seem likely to make a purchase themselves during their visit to the restaurant. At the very least, Pizza Hut has leveraged the classroom to get inside students' homes. Campbell's Soup features a "Labels for Education" program that encourages students to collect and redeem Campbell proof of purchases so that participating schools can redeem them for free merchandise. This program today reaches 75,000 schools and organizations and more than 42 million students. Over the thirty year life of the program Campbell's has provided more than $100 million in merchandise to America's schools. (About the Program, 2007) Proctor and Gamble offers a "Crest Healthy Smiles 1st Grade Dental health Program" to motivate kids and parents to take care of their teeth and gums. The program includes Crest toothpaste samples, Glide floss, and brochures and educational pamphlets with the Crest logo. (P & G School Programs, 2007) In 2003 the Field Trip Factory organized 3,300 field trips to Petco, where students get to learn about animal characteristics and their habitats. Kids on this trip receive a goodie bag which includes a store coupon. Parents often return back to the store with their children to see what the kids saw on the trip and redeem their coupon. (Hightower, 2003) Cover Concepts, a division of Marvel Entertainment, has been providing free

45

educational materials to schools since 1989. But the school supplies are emblazoned with corporate logos and cartoon characters. (Cover Concepts, 2007)

Other numerous corporate programs targeted at schools exist. The point is to not necessarily question the educational value of these programs but rather to examine if companies are ethical in targeting these programs to children in schools. Companies may believe that since they outlay a great deal of money for educational programs that they should at least be recognized and receive some form of payback in return for their educational investments. What efforts have been made to reconcile corporate investment in the public school system while reasonably limiting the amount and impact of marketing on this captive, impressionable audience? In one case, school administrators, teachers, and parents worked together to arrive at ethical standards in deciding which materials to use. Two middle schools teamed up with students trained in media literacy from a nearby state university to teach students how to be media savvy. The college students taught the middle school students how to look at ads with a critical eye and to consider what the company is selling, why it's targeted to kids and how kids might be influenced by the ad. (McAulay, 2006)

Rising obesity rates among America's children represents another issue that has been linked with unethical marketing practices. One study of youth marketing professionals expressed conflicted reasoning on this issue:

> "On the issue of child obesity, while 97% of youth-oriented professionals feel that youth obesity is at least a 'somewhat important' public health issue (with 50% deeming it 'extremely important') a full 68% are reticent to blame food companies as the 'primary' factor in the issue, and 69% said 'health and well-being' should be a matter of personal responsibility. Assigning such responsibility becomes problematic, however, when advertising begins years before one's capacity for critical thought." (Grimm, 2004)

Junk food has been recently promoted to children through a wide range of promotional digital techniques such as targeting kids with mobile marketing campaigns that encourage kids to text message an exclusive phone number to receive special coupons or premiums. These techniques represent still one more way to cut parents out of the marketing communication. (Olsen, 2007) Other promotions include using bright packaging, intensely colored and flavored ingredients, free gifts, and links between cartoon characters, pop stars, sporting heroes, and popular children's films. (Dalmeny, 2003) One Department of Agriculture study calculated that 95% of the 10,000 commercials children see market high-fat, high-sugar products. Commercials for candy, snacks, and fast food have been demonstrated to effectively persuade children's preference for the advertised products. One study reported in the Wall Street Journal examined groups of five to seven year old kids. One group watched ten toy ads after watching a cartoon and then two weeks later watched a cartoon that was followed by food ads. After the kids watched the food ads, they ended up eating up to 17% more calories than after seeing the toy ads. Even more revealing was that a group of nine to eleven year olds ate up to 134% more calories after being exposed to the food ads compared with their snack intake after watching the toy ads. (Parker-Pope) This finding is particularly significant given that commercials for unhealthy foods far outnumber the commercials for nutritious foods. Eating habits formed during childhood often persist throughout life which further gives emphasis to the serious implications of marketer's potential unethical influences on children. (Kunkel, Wilcox, Cantor, Palmer, Linn, & Dowrick, 2004)

The Theory of Reasoned Action (TORA) that was outlined in chapter 2 represents another potential unethical approach to marketing to children Many companies leverage their marketing by encouraging kids to exert normative influences over each other. Fulfilling the need to belong, the need to be cool, to be popular, and to be accepted by one's peers can exert powerful economic and commercial influences that persuade a child to purchase particular products. Social status often expressed through what kids wear and the items they own encourages other children to want similar items. Branding products at an earlier and earlier age has become paramount to many companies. This is now evidenced

47

by the fact that by the time children are 36 months old, they recognize 100 brand logos. (Zoll, 2000) By the time they're three years old, most American children start making specific requests for name brand products. (Tips for Parenting in a Commercial Culture, 2002) Children are entering formal social situations earlier in life than previous generations. One marketer claims that when children enter kindergarten they start being influenced by their peers. (Nestoras, 2001) Do normative influences work? One study of children reported that six out of ten kids feel pressure to buy stuff to fit in. (Chatzky, 2003)

One of the key marketing techniques to employ the TORA model is viral marketing. Viral marketing represents an organized approach to creating a buzz that encourages kids to talk to each other while once again cutting out parents from the marketing communication channel. The internet represents a prime communication channel to create buzz. According to a survey of 100 school principals and administrators commercial web sites pose a greater threat to students than pornographic web sites. Only an estimated 2% of children's web sites are commercial free. (Rowings, 2007) The Children's Online Privacy Protection Act prohibits companies from directly emailing to children under age 13 without parental permission. But, marketers can and do encourage kids to email each other. As part of Disneyland's 50th anniversary, Disney used a technique called advergaming, or placing advertising within an online game. Disney set up a free interactive, multiplayer game called "Virtual Magic Kingdom" that aimed to provide a free virtual visit to any of Disney's global resorts and theme parks. The games are based on attractions at the theme parks. The games were also used to create buzz about the anniversary celebration among the target market of eight to twelve year olds and then to encourage kids to urge their parents to visit a Disney theme park. ('Advergames' Target Tween Market, 2005) Nabisco features an online web site, Nabiscoworld, complete with games contains that prominently display their brand logos and where you can refer a friend to the gaming site. (Nabiscoworld) Mountain Dew features a sophisticated gaming site where you can tell a friend about the game you played.

One game features a tie in to the movie "Transformers," complete with a vending machine that transforms into an alien robot with a mission to complete. (Mountain Dew)

Sometimes kids are personally recruited to generate buzz. One youth marketing firm cultivates eight year old girls who serve in the role of influencing other girls by sponsoring a slumber party at the influencer's house. A box packed with goodies such as accessories and games is provided at the slumber party with the hope that the peer dynamics will encourage the girls to try and talk about the products and spread the word. (Marketing to "Tweens" Going Too Far?, 2007)

The Reaction of the Marketing Industry

A contrasting view of marketing to children may be found in Europe. The European Union adopted "The Television without Frontiers" directive in 1989.[3] One of its clauses states that television advertising must not directly entice minors to buy by taking advantage of their inexperience. Each European country may enact measures to follow the standards of this directive. The governments of Sweden and Norway prohibit television advertising that directly target children under age 12. Greece bans TV stations from advertising toys to children between the hours of 7 A.M. and 10 P.M. Luxembourg and Belgium prohibit children's advertising five minutes before and after children's programs. In Italy, commercials may not interrupt cartoons. (Dumont, 2001) Quebec restricts all television advertising directed at children under the age of 13. (Zoll, 2000) By contrast, the United States views marketing products to children as a First Amendment right as a freedom of speech issue.

Youth marketing professionals in the United States recognize the issues discussed in this chapter and expressed their concern in a 2004 poll in which those surveyed said 91% of kids are marketed to in ways they don't notice and 61% believe that advertising to children starts too young. The survey respondents also thought that children cannot effectively separate fantasy from reality before

---

[3] This directive was modified in 1997 and is under review in 2007.

49

age 9 or make intelligent purchase decisions before age 12; yet a majority of the survey respondents also felt that they could start marketing to children at age 7. (Fonda & Roston, 2004) Most leaders in the marketing profession recognize the need to take responsibility in recognizing that advertising standards for children should be different than for adults.

Many companies appear to be disconnected from their marketing tactics to children and the results of those tactics. A survey of professional youth marketers found that 47% of the respondents stated that schools should be a protected area, and we should not be advertising to children on school grounds; but at the same time, 74% said they expect to see more advertising there in the future. Companies must address these disconnects in a proactive manner or face serious consequences from angry parents and other concerned individuals. As one marketer stated "Our industry must be less defensive or we invite regulation. Too often we put our own business needs ahead of the needs of children and the two don't need to be exclusive." (Grimm, 2004)

The Reaction of Third Parties

Organizations have stepped forward to argue the merits of child marketing as long as 100 years ago. In 1929, The National Education Association (NEA) argued that corporate sponsored materials should in general be used only if they are indispensable to the education of children. (Broome, 1929) In 1990, Consumers Union called for making schools ad free zones, where children can pursue learning without commercial influences and pressures. They strongly stated that:

- All forms of advertising in classrooms is inappropriate and not an acceptable way of marketing to children.
- While schools are under financed and can benefit from the resources of the business community, businesses should assist schools with programs whose objectives are empowering and educating youth, not selling to them.

50

- Educational communities adopt ethical guidelines that require sponsored programs and materials to undergo review procedures and to meet the same standards as other curriculum materials.
- School systems identify and pursue noncommercial partnerships with business.
- Children should be educated about the nature of commercial messages by teaching media literacy, helping kids to analyze ads and evaluate sources of information.
- That tax benefits for corporate contributions to schools that carry a commercial message be eliminated.

The Consumers Union continues on to state "That all sponsored materials designed for educational use be clearly designated as such. Text and illustrations must not contain any of the sponsor's brand names or corporate identification. No implied or explicit sales message, exhortation to buy a product or service, merchandising slogan or other attempts to influence the purchasing decisions of pupils, or their families should be included." (Captive Kids: A Report on Commercial Pressures on Kids at School, 1990)

In 2004, the Seattle School Board, facing pressures from many concerned groups, approved a comprehensive set of nutrition related policies designed to provide students with healthy food and beverage choices. All Seattle schools would no longer sell any foods containing high levels of sugar and fat and prohibit exclusive vendor beverage contracts. In addition, the new policies require all food and beverages sold and distributed during the school day to meet the Seattle School District's nutrition and portion guidelines. (Seattle School Board Approves Comprehensive Suite of Nutrition Policies, 2004)

Other school systems are trying a different technique to control children's food selections. Primero Food Service Solutions allows parents to set up prepaid lunch accounts so children don't have to carry money. The system also allows parents to control their child's food selections. This program has been successfully implanted in schools systems in Texas, Arizona, Oklahoma,

Michigan, and Tennessee. (What Do Houston Kids Eat? Parent Are Watching, 2006)

Commercial Alert, an organization who claims their mission is to keep commercial culture from exploiting children and protect family values, states that they are especially concerned with the use of electronic media to bypass parents and speak directly to impressionable children. Commercial Alert is presently appealing to members of Congress to create a "Parents' Bill of Rights," a series of proposed legislative acts that includes banning advertising in schools, proper food labeling, labeling product placements in media, privacy safeguards, and a total ban of television advertising to children under twelve years old. A complete copy of the proposed Parents' Bill of Rights may be found in the appendix. (Rowe & Ruskin)

The American Academy of Pediatrics recently moved forward with a policy statement that calls on Congress to impose extensive limits on television ads that target children. The group demands that television ads on kids' shows be cut in half and that junk food ads be banned during shows viewed predominately by those under age eight. This same group urged Congress to convene a national task force to propose solutions toward limiting children's exposure to unhealthy advertising. (Teinowitz, 2006)

In December 2005, the Institute of Medicine called on food and beverage manufacturers and restaurants to make more healthful products and shift their advertising emphasis to promote them. If the companies refused to do so within two years, the Institute recommended that Congress mandate changes, especially for broadcast and cable ads. The report stated "There is strong evidence that exposure to television advertising is associated with obesity." The report said that most food and beverage products promoted to children are high in calories, sugar, salt, and fat and low in nutrients.

In the summer of 2007 the Federal Trade Commission plans to examine child marketing practices. Besides television advertising, The FTC intends to review the use of product placement, advertising of food and beverages in schools, and on-line interactive advertising. (Rules to Restrict Ads Aimed at Youths, 2007)

The Responsibility of Youth Marketers

Youth marketers must take initiative by recognizing that they need to think about the welfare of the children they target. They can respond to criticisms by trying to gain the trust of parents and to create positive interaction between parents and child. The Direct Marketing Association advocates that no child under 16 be marketed to without the direct permission of a parent or guardian. (Nicholas, 2006) Some restaurants and fast food operations are attempting to introduce alternative healthy menu selections that can still make them money. Can they find a way to make healthy food choice rather than chocolate seem cool? Other companies are taking notice and launching initiatives to promote healthier lifestyles:

- On July 18, 2007, eleven of the nation's biggest food and drink companies adopted new rules to voluntarily limit advertising to children younger than twelve. The eleven companies account for approximately two thirds of the television food ads directed to children. Included in the rules are pledges by seven of the companies to no longer use licensed characters on television, internet, or print media. (Rules to Restrict Ads Aimed at Youths, 2007)
- Kraft has introduced an educational meal program in schools and has introduced a "Sensible Solution" line of products that meet FDA nutritional standards that will be used on web sites targeting kids age 6-11.
- Coca-Cola and McDonald's have launched fitness programs.
- Frito-Lay has looked to bolster its reputation through healthier food offerings.

- PepsiCo has reallocated half of its advertising budget toward 100 "Smart Spot" products, foods that meet FDA and National Academy of Science standards. PepsiCo also placed on its website parental information on teaching children how to live a healthier lifestyle.
- Nabisco is moving to controlled portion snacks, such as 100 calorie packs, and adding healthier, organic items to their product line.
- Unilever's Knorr brand now offers pasta and rice side dishes made from whole grains. (Reyes, 2006)
- In the summer of 2007, Kellogg announced that they won't promote foods on television, radio, print, or web sites that reach audiences at least half of whom are under age 12 unless a single serving of the product contains no more than 200 calories, no transfat, no more than two grams of saturated fat, no more than 230 milligrams of sodium, and no more than twelve grams of sugar. Kellogg also said it would reformulate products to meet these criteria or stop marketing them to children under 12 by the end of 2008. (Kellogg Won't Market Sugary Cereal to Children, 2007)

The industry has historically tried to self regulate itself. The Children's Advertising Review Unit (CARU) of the Council of the Better Business Bureau was founded in 1974 to promote responsible children's advertising as part of a strategic alliance with the major advertising trade associations. CARU sets standards for the advertising industry to assure that advertising directed to children is not deceptive, unfair, or inappropriate for its intended audience. CARU states their guidelines "…take into account the special vulnerabilities of children, e.g., their inexperience, immaturity, susceptibility to being misled or unduly influenced, and their lack of cognitive skills to evaluate the credibility of advertising." (Self-Regulatory Program for Children's Advertising, 2006) In particular, CARU monitors and reviews advertising directed to children. CARU also initiates and receives complaints about advertising practices and determines whether the practices violate the program's standards. While critics argue that CARU is toothless and ineffective. Elizabeth Lascoutx, CARU's director, responds by stating that her staff has been effective. From 2003-2005, CARU asked companies to revise 254 ads and only six refused. CARU's core principles and guidelines are located in the appendix.

Marketers can also ethically improve the impact of marketing to impressionable minds by carefully separating reality from fantasy in their advertising. Promoters should consider child marketing to create an opportunity for consumer learning. In particular, companies should consider marketing to children in a way that marketers would feel good about if the message was being viewed by their own children. Failure to do so may mean that legislation and regulations may in the end severely restrict legitimate efforts to effectively serve this market.

Chapter 5

How Much Is Too Much? - The Materialistic American Culture

"I am my Mercedes. I am my Apple. I am my Big Mac. I am my Nikes. I am my MTV. We are cars, we are computers, we are what we eat and wear and watch. The end effect of the ethos is the eradication of significant differences among consumers, people who are inasmuch as they are consumers are clones."

- Benjamin R. Barber

Why Is Materialism a Problem?

The World Book Dictionary's definition of "consume" includes terms such as "devour," "destroy," and "waste." Describing consumers using up the world's resources in this manner sounds alarming. Even more alarming is that the World Book Dictionary defines materialism as "an ethical doctrine that material self-interest should and does determine conduct." Individuals pursuing happiness do so through acquisitions rather than through experiences, personal relationships, or achievement. People who are into a materialistic lifestyle tend to judge their own and other's success by the number and quality of their accumulated possessions. In essence, Americans have evolved into materialists who are in essence motivated by their economic well being. Given that marketers by nature encourage people to purchase and consume, the implications of Americans' consumption on our world must be examined along with the marketing profession's role in encouraging consumption. (The World Book Dictionary, 1985)

Consumptionism was first coined by the political philosopher Samuel Strauss in 1925. According to Strauss, consumptionism involved a commitment to produce and consume more things from one year to the next. All values were subordinated to emphasize one's standard of living. This concept emphasized the pressures business interests brought to bear on people to consume. Businesses shifted from a strategy of providing consumers what they wanted to compelling consumers to want and need what the business was producing and selling. Cultural values became focused on acquiring and consuming as the means to achieve happiness. Money value became the predominant measure of all value in society. (Leach, 1993)

Two-thirds of the United State's economy is driven by consumer spending. Because forty percent of this spending is discretionary in nature, in theory Americans first decide if they wish to spend and if so, they next decide on what items to purchase, how much they wish to spend on those items, and where to shop for their purchases. Exhibit 5-1 demonstrates how consumers spend their discretionary income and the four categories of purchases that result from their shopping decisions:

- **Utilitarian Purchase** – Consists of products that while consumers do not stringently need, will improve their lives. Examples include practical problem solving or time saving appliances such as microwave ovens or vacuum cleaners.

- **Lifestyle Luxuries** – Products that offer utility and usefulness along with prestige, image, and superior quality often denoted through a brand name. Examples include designer clothes and upscale automobiles.

- **Indulgences** – Small luxuries that consumers purchase that provide emotional gratification with little guilt. Indulgences include music, flowers, chocolate, and hobby purchases.

- **Aspirational Luxuries** – represented by purchases that allow consumers to express their values, interests, and passions. Original art, boats, and fine jewelry represent examples of product in this category. (Danziger, 2002)

58

Exhibit 5-1

Discretionary Products Matrix

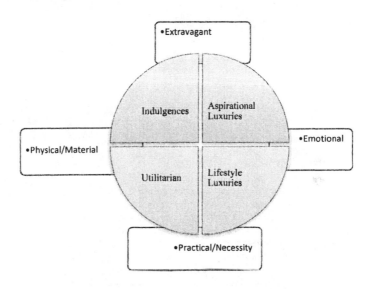

Source: "Why People Buy Things They Don't Need" by Pamela N. Danziger

Exhibit 5-2 provides reasons why consumers justify spending their discretionary income.

All these decisions are subject to many businesses sales pitches. A materialism view suggests that the American culture, lacking spiritualism, tries to address many needs through shopping and purchasing items that they hope will make themselves feel fulfilled. More Americans visit shopping malls each week than attend houses of worship. (Graaf, Wann, & Naylor, 2001) Consumers attempt to rationalize their decisions but typically purchase discretionary products primarily based on emotion. Many retailers recognize the need to appeal to people's emotional needs through what George Ritzer, Professor of Sociology at the University of Maryland, describes as "cathedrals of consumption," stores that have an enchanted, sacred religious character for people. Ritzer goes on to suggest that "In order for retailers to attract ever-larger numbers of consumers, such cathedrals of consumption need to offer increasingly magical, fantastic, and enchanted settings in which to consume."

Exhibit 5-2

Justifiers for Buying Discretionary Products

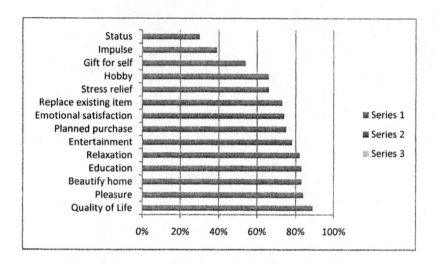

Source: "Why People Buy Things They Don't Need" by Pamela N. Danziger

Shopping malls have come to fulfill many of the same needs a church used to: social contact with others, walking in nature (witness the sophisticated use of trees and plants in most malls), and to participate in a form of holiday festivals. Fulfilling consumer needs allows these "cathedrals of consumption" to spend more on goods and services. (Ritzer, 1999)

Consumption then may be seen as a means to help people define who they are. Social status revolves around consumption; in essence, consumers buy a lifestyle. The products purchased to fit the chosen lifestyle is based on the need to fit in (remember the Theory of Reasoned Action from chapter 2). The heavy marketing of fashion and brand names in essence push consumers to purchase products that they may not need to simply fit in with the lifestyle and social status they seek. To deal with social pressures, people will often purchase additional products to feel better about their selves. One home improvement retailer advertises "Want the best yard in the block?" Malls and stores are designed to create moods to encourage buying. All this consumption in turns creates financial stresses on individuals and impacts the world's environment.

Why Should Marketers Be Concerned?

Given this brief background on how and why American consumers spend their discretionary income, why does the marketing profession need to be concerned with the American materialistic culture? After all, don't consumers have free will? Can't consumers decide to save rather than spend their discretionary income? When they do decide to purchase products, don't consumers have free will on what to purchase? Should marketers give people what they want even if what they want isn't good for them? These questions are best viewed through the impacts of American's lifestyle choices on our culture, finances, and resource usage.

America has become a nation of shoppers. Shopping has become embedded in the American culture. In 1987 the number of shopping centers in the country surpassed the number of schools. Americans used vacations to shop. The nation's largest shopping center, the Mall of America, represents the country's biggest tourist attraction. The amount of retail space has quadrupled over the last thirty years. Mayor Rudolph Giuliani's attempt to establish normalcy following the terrible tragedy of September 11, 2001 counseled Americans not to stay at home with our families or pray but instead to go shopping. (Zukin, 2004) Jeb Bush, the Florida Governor, was even more explicit, stating:

> "We need to respond quickly so people regain confidence and consider it their patriotic duty to go shopping, go to a restaurant, take a cruise, travel

61

with their family. Frankly, the terrorists win if Americans don't go back to normalcy."

Because we shop everyday, Mayor Giuliani and Governor Bush understood that shopping equated with normalcy in Americans' lives.

What drives Americans to shop and spend so much? People often believe that purchasing products will make them happy. Advertisers often make people feel that people must constantly replace old or outdated items with fresh ones. One major home improvement company recently ran a radio ad with the following lines:

Male Consumer: "I love my old power tools. They've helped me with so many home projects"

Announcer: "We are now featuring 10% off all new power tools."

Male Consumer: "Man, I hate my old power tools."

Or consider this actual radio advertisement"

Wife: "Come here and check out the refrigerator."

Husband: "What is it? Oh my"

Wife: "That's right. Our refrigerator is ugly."

Announcer: "Tire of dated appliances? Come check out the latest lines at _____ ."

Consumers believe that purchasing products will make them happy. Oddly the opposite has proven true. The reality is that the more consumers purchase, the less happy they become. The percentage of Americans who described themselves as happy actually peaked in 1957 and has fallen steadily over the last half century despite the fact that Americans have twice as many possessions as they did then. (Graaf, Wann, & Naylor, 2001) Other studies show that people with materialistic values are less satisfied with life, experience more anxiety, experience poorer relationships, contribute less to their communities, and tend to have more anti-social behaviors. (Kasser, 2001)

The most evident manifestation of American materialism is represented by the rise of "McMansions," houses with at least four bedrooms. Houses with five or more rooms were the fastest growing type between 1990 and 2005. In the 1950's the average house size was 950 square feet. Over the next 50 years the average U.S. house size grew to 2,434 square feet. Many of these new homes include an attached three to four bay garage. This demand for larger homes came as the country's average household size shrunk to 2.6 people. American homes are almost twice as large as those in many European countries. Along with these larger homes comes the increased need for land, building materials, sewer, water, and of course, enough possessions to fill the house up. (Peake, 2007) Even more astonishing, despite the growth of larger homes, the storage unit business represents a high growth industry in the United States. More than 30,000 self-storage facilities offering over a billion feet exist in the U.S. (Kidd, 2000) Despite the larger homes, Americans still have too many possessions and need to rent additional storage space.

A Theoretical Perspective of Materialism

The social comparison theory suggests that Americans feel a need to keep up. In the mid twentieth century, people would follow the social norms of their work circle and neighborhood; these associative reference groups consisted of people and households of similar incomes and means. These reference groups

63

can exert tremendous pressures on their members. Nearly six out of ten kids say they feel pressure to buy stuff to fit in. (Chatzky, Parties Without the Presents, 2003) Today, consumers seek out luxuries found in aspirational reference group lifestyles of the affluent and upper middle income. Researchers have found that people can tell one's social status by looking at what that person drives, the clothes he or she wears, and the type of house they own. With more social openness, conspicuous consumption becomes more acceptable at all levels. (Schor J. B., 1998)

Companies encourage consumers to seek indulgences, lifestyle luxuries, and aspirational luxuries by making products more identifiable in their marketing campaigns. According to the designer Tommy Hilfiger:

> "I can't sell a shirt without a logo. If I put a shirt without a logo on my selling floor next to a shirt with a logo – same shirt, same color, same price – the one with the logo will blow it out. It will sell 10 times over the one without the logo. It's a status thing as well. It really is." (Schor J. B., 1998)

These marketing cues and communications help people emulate the social identity and class they seek. Consumers find themselves comparing themselves to the celebrity lifestyle they see in the media. Professionals such as wealthy businesspeople, doctors, lawyers, and other upper and upper middle class professionals predominate on television while blue collar and low status occupations tend to be underrepresented as compared with their numbers in the real world. These television characters use consumption symbols as a means of visual shorthand. Their possessions and the activities they participate in mark their social status. Viewers see and hear how members of the affluent upper social classes lead their lives and how they consume. Television programs may be seen as blurring fictional with reality that consumers passively accept as real, creating consumption-related social expectations. (O'Guinn & Shrum, 1997) As a consequence, consumers spend a great deal of their discretionary income on purchasing products to simply identify their social status. The result is that

64

consumers engage in competitive spending, trying to keep up with everyone else who also at the same time are trying to upscale to feel a part of their aspirational reference group. One outcome from this is that Americans spend more money than necessary on brands simply to project a status that they may not be capable to financially afford.

Consequences of American Materialism

As credit card technology has become more prevalent and easier for consumers to use, consumer debt has rapidly escalated in the past decade. Over 6,000 credit card issuers exist with some rates as high as forty percent. An average household now pays more than $800 in penalty fees and interest each year – a total of $90 billion annually. (Bennett, 2006) One estimate places consumer credit card debt in 2007 at well over $1 trillion, an increase of 225% over the last ten years. (Credit Card Debt Consumer Crisis Looms , 2007)

An "I want it now" attitude appears to be pervasive among American consumers today. In 1952, household debt to disposable income was less than forty percent. In 2007, this ratio stood at 126 percent. In essence, households are spending more than they earn. (Bennett, Q & A: Why Consumer Debt is Rising, 2006) About 42% of 18 to 49 year olds said they would are likely to spend more than they can afford. Because of so much consumer spending, national personal savings rates was a negative one percent for 2006, the worst showing in 73 years. In essence, consumers are dipping into their savings to finance current spending. (Americans Lack Money Cushion, 2007)

In order to seek growth, many credit card companies seek out younger markets – as young as three years old. Cards such as PAYjr and Visa Buxx, targeted to children as young as 13, teach kids to use credit cards before they recognize the ramifications of a buy now, pay later mentality. One out of ten teens uses credit cards. The debts incurred accrue through college. The average graduating senior carries an average of four credit cards and $3,000 in credit card debt. (Meet Generation Plastic, 2007) This trend continued on after graduation.

One survey reported that adults between the ages of 25 and 34 hold an average credit card debt of almost $4,400. Because of the high college loan and consumer debt credit loads, 58% of college graduates moved back home after college; more than 32% stayed at home for over a year. (Grads Boomerang Back to Parents, 2006)

Not all credit card usage is bad. Credit cards provide resources for consumer emergencies, access to financial funds that can be used at any time virtually anywhere in the world. How consumers use credit cards become the issue. Consumers respond to a buy now, pay later advertising theme. A major soft drink company started accepting credit cards as payments at their vending machines. They found that consumers who paid with their credit cards spent 32% more than cash customers. Daniel Howard, Chair of the Marketing Department at Southern Methodist University's Cox School of Business says "If you're not even signing your name, there's no commitment, and that increases impulse purchasing." (Got Cash? Plastic Gains Ground, 2007)

Possibly more critical than materialism's impact on the individual and society is the harm caused to the world's environment. American's materialistic lifestyles entail an enormous and continuous dependence on commodities that generate the most damage to the earth to produce: energy, chemicals metal, and paper. American's appetite for the wood and minerals used to build "McMansions" and fill them with possessions open tropical rain forests to development that drives many species to extinction. Larger homes use more energy and increase the use of toxic chemicals. Many of the minerals exported to the United States come from countries that do not have the environmental laws that are regulated in America. (Durning, 1993)

With less than five percent of the world's population, the United States consumes nearly thirty percent of the global resources. Industry moves, mines, extracts, wastes, and disposes of four million pounds of material in order to provide one average middle class family's needs for a year. The typical American discards about a ton of trash per year and Americans spend more for

66

trash bags alone than ninety of the world's countries spend for everything. Per person, Americans consume forty percent of the world's gasoline. (Taylor B. , 2000) In an average lifetime, each American will consume forty three million gallons of water and 2,500 barrels of oil. Americans consume one third of the world's wood. American vehicles annually burn 155 billion gallons of oil, generate a quarter of the nation's greenhouse gas, and create 7 billion pounds of unrecycled scrap and waste. Americans generate enough solid waste to fill a convoy of garbage trucks that would stretch halfway to the moon. (Graaf, Wann, & Naylor, 2001) An Earth Council Study indicated that if everyone on Earth consumed as much as Americans do, four extra planets would be needed to supply the resources and absorb the waste. (Taylor B. , 2000)

The Responsibility of the Marketing Profession

The marketing profession must examine their role in creating an American culture of materialism. In "The Overspent American," sociologist Juliet Schor discusses the impact of advertising on consumer status identification. She suggests that marketers encode messages beyond the product itself. Research demonstrates how brand image can be used to position a product by creating symbolic meanings on who should consume their brand, in what circumstances the product should be used, and how the product should be consumed. A previous chapter on marketing to children indicated these encoded messages are learned at an early age. The clothing one wears clearly communicates one's social standing. Even the frequency of how often clothes are worn may ascertain a person's social status. Wearing the same clothes to the office becomes a social taboo. The right clothing must be selected for special occasions, trips to a sporting event, or to a job interview. (Schor J. B., 1998)

Previous chapters covered the extent that these marketing communications intrude into our lives in such a prevalent manner. The level of advertising pitched to Americans invades consumers' psyche and is pervasive throughout our society. What can be done to create a more healthy perspective

67

toward our materialistic lifestyle? This question is important for marketers to consider, because if the profession cannot regulate itself, then either government or consumer social movements may take matters out of the profession's hands. Kalle Lasn, author of Culture Jam, represents one extreme view. He advocates people to resist by toppling existing power structures and to foster major adjustments to the way people live in the 21st century. He suggests a grass roots approach through disrupting businesses and in essence getting consumers to act as a combination idealist and anarchist. (Barber, 2007) A consumer civil right's movement would engage direct consumer action such as demonstrations and boycotts. The goal of these consumer advocate groups is to exert economic pressure on companies to change the way they market and conduct their business. One example is the Council on Economic Priorities (CEP), a public interest research group encourages consumers to use their purchasing power as a vote to express preferences through an economic means. CEP publishes a consumer guide that rates companies on their environmental performance, charitable donations, community outreach programs, and information disclosure policies. (Cohen, Comrove, & Hoffner, 2005) One parent created a toy recycling web site that allows children to trade their toys rather than simply purchasing new toys. (Web Site Lets 1 Kid's Trash Be Another Kid's Treasure, 2006) Some consumer advocates argue that people need to be better educated as to the consequences of their purchase decision making. Others suggest that more government regulation is needed:

- To ensure that the true cost of a good or service is reflected in product purchase prices. The true price would reflect the cost to the environment to produce, use, and dispose of the product. This might occur through the introduction of use taxes or fees.
- To create product labels that reflects meaningful information regarding the impact in energy and raw materials to produce that particular product. The belief is that informed consumers would

68

be in position to exercise better judgment on their purchase and consumption of products.

- More emphasis on truth in advertising so that consumers will receive fair, relevant information on which to base their decisions. (Gibbons, 2000)

Most business may become more cooperative and willing to address the ethical concerns regarding their role in promoting American materialism. Consumer and government external forces on industry may encourage self-regulation rather than to have formal government regulation imposed. Some practices are already changing, such as warning labels on children's video games and fast food restaurants' response to consumer pressures by adding healthier meal alternatives to their menus.

This chapter's topic raises an interesting ethical dilemma for marketers. Marketing by its very nature is supposed to address consumer demand. In a capitalist free-market society materialism breeds competitiveness and is a major driver for companies to innovate and improve product performance. But the United States cannot continue consuming at current rates. Marketers play a role in this excess and therefore on some level must take some of the responsibility. However, in a capitalistic free market economy this may prove to be difficult without some form of external intervention. Hopefully consumers, government, and industry can find a way to work together for effective voluntary self-regulation.

Chapter 6

Body Image Advertising: Do Today's Models Promote Unhealthy Body Images?

"When women are asked what they most wish for, the vast majority say 'to lose weight' – not to make lots of money, have love in their lives, be successful, or have the world at peace. This is a tragic failure of imagination."

> - *Jean Kilbourne*

The Power of Marketing

Media power is strong and should never be underestimated. A Harvard researcher demonstrated some interesting findings on the impact of television on women's feelings about their body types. A survey of high school girls in Nadroga, Fiji, was taken 38 months after television arrived. High scores on a test indicating risk for eating disorders were significantly more frequent among the schoolgirls than prior to the arrival of television on the island. Those who watched television at least three nights a week were 50% more likely to see themselves as too fat and 30% more likely to diet, although the more frequent television watchers were not more overweight. As one Fiji girl stated:

> "We can see [teenagers] on TV ... They are the same ages, but they are working, they are slim and tall, and they are cute, nice. We want our bodies to become like that. So we try to lose a lot of weight."

Traditionally, Fijians have preferred robust body shapes, reflecting the importance placed on eating generous servings. (Reynolds, 1999)

71

Media and the marketing industry have been accused of portraying certain body types as attractive which causes body dissatisfaction and consequently decisions by people that harm their bodies. Marketing and media present society's conception of the idealized male and female; traits that most cannot achieve. A study of 4,294 network television commercials revealed that 1 out of every 3.8 commercials contained an attractiveness message, telling viewers what is or is not attractive. (The Media, Body Image, and Eating Disorders, 2002) Studies indicate that marketers influence consumers' views of body standards by promoting an ideal for visual appearance in American society. Women and men see these flawless bodies and strive to live up to the images because they feel these pictures represent reality. If people feel they don't measure up to the idealized body image, they may feel dissatisfied. This chapter will first cover the impact of unrealistic body images on women and later the more recent developments on the consequences of the Adonis images on men.

Nature of Body Image Issue for Women

Appearance is an important factor for women in developing positive self-esteem. (Mazur, 1986) Women in the United States feel pressured to measure up to certain social and cultural ideal standards of beauty. Media exposure has been found to constrain women's conceptions of femininity by putting appearance and physical attractiveness at the center of women's values. Women in particular are bombarded by media images of female bodies that are extremely thin and with flawless features. They cite the media as the most important source of pressure to be thin. (Levitt, 1997) In commercials, women are portrayed as glamorous, attractive, and sexually desirable only if they are young and thin. As a consequence, women often feel unhappy with their appearance and may pursue unhealthy behaviors ranging from eating disorders to unnecessary cosmetic surgery.

Researchers indicate this impacts both the models and on the consumers who take in the images of these models. Women report more dissatisfaction with their bodies than men. During the 1970's as the current trend in slender models was well underway, women described an attractive female body as slim, small buttocks, and middle to small busts. (Horvath, 1981) Women report that they perceive themselves to be heavier than they actually are and feel a desire to be thinner.   Not surprising, women also think the ideal body size is significantly thinner than their perceived actual body size. (Cohn & Addler, 1992)

On average, an American woman views approximately 3,000 advertisements every day. (Kilbourne, 2002). In many of these advertisements "beautiful" models who appear tall and thin and are used to sell products. While only 9% of television commercials directly sell beauty, nearly 50% of advertising targeting girls refer to beauty and physical attractiveness to sell products. (Eating Disorders: Body Imaging and Advertising) One out of four commercials refers to what is or is not attractive. (The Media, Body Image and Eating Disorders) A recent bottled water ad suggested "If you could choose your own body, which body would you choose?" The body images in the ad were all tanned, toned, and thin. In essence, the superthin models used in marketing represent an aspirational reference group that is highly unattainable for most women. Sometimes the ads are more subtle. A national hotel chain ran a print ad that showed parents and their son on vacation at a beach. The mother appears to be so thin that her rib cage is visibly evident.

The value of slimness represents a recent shift in the beauty ideas in America. Waif-look models were not always in vogue. In the 1950's larger women (and in particular large busted women), such as Marilyn Monroe (who was a size 14), represented the ideal of feminine beauty. Oddly, the trend toward slenderness has often been associated with feminists starting in the 1960's. Ads such as the distinct image of an emancipated woman smoking Virginia Slims showed women succeeding at work and with men by having a stylishly slim figure. The 1960's also brought about the mini-skirt which promoted the slender hips and legs of fashion models. Skinny models such as Twiggy became popular. The introduction of designer jeans in the 1970's further emphasized the move to slender hips and smaller buttocks. The 1980's saw a move away from supermodels such as Cheryl Tiegs to waif thin celebrity models like Kate Moss, who stands 5'7" and weighs 95 pounds, or 30% below ideal body weight.. Today's fashion models weigh 23% less than the average female. A woman between the ages of 18-34 has only a 7% chance of being as thin as a supermodel. (The Media and Eating Disorders) The gap between actual body sizes and the cultural ideal is getting wider, causing anxiety among almost all women.

Marketing images contribute to women's feelings of body dissatisfaction. Ads that employ slender models shape the body images of women. One study demonstrated that females exhibited greater dissatisfaction with their bodies after viewing media stereotypical pictures of attractive women. (Ogden & Mundray, 1996) Depression and loss of self-esteem may be indirectly facilitated by these ads. A psychological study found that three minutes spent looking at models in fashion magazines caused 70% of women to feel depressed, guilty, and shameful. (Women's Health) Store mannequins typically are eight inches taller 6 inches smaller in the waist and hips, and several dress sizes than the average American woman. (Impossibly Thin?, 2005)

Reinforcing the pressure to be thin are numerous ads that push the concept that thin is glamorous and attractive. Consider that over fifty percent of young women between the ages of 11 to 15 years old read fashion and beauty related magazines. One in three articles in these magazines include a focus on appearance and 50% of the advertisements in these magazines use a beauty appeal to sell their products. A Harvard research study found that 67% of girls who were frequent readers of fashion magazines in fifth through twelfth grades are more likely to diet or exercise to lose weight. Furthermore, 69% of the girls said pictures in magazines influence their idea of an ideal body. Women's magazines have ten times more ads and articles promoting weight loss than men's magazines do, and over three quarters of women's magazines include at least one message about how to achieve a better body. (McWhorter, 2003)

Marketing Body Image to Young Girls

Girls at a young age are conditioned to achieve a waif look. In the 1950's, girls played with baby dolls they nurtured and cared for. Then along came Barbie, the first doll to represent an adult figure in a child's life. Barbie turned into a role model to emulate, a young woman who had it all. Barbie became a leader in what was to become a new standard of female figure beauty. However, Barbie's dimensions are totally unrealistic. If she were alive, Barbie would stand seven feet tall with a waistline of 18 inches, hips of 33-35 inches, and a bust line of 38-40 inches. She would weigh only 110 pounds, thinner than most anorexics and physically unable to menstruate. Her body would be too narrow to contain more than half a liver and a few centimeters of bowel. She would most likely be unable to walk erect. Her feet, pointed to fit into high-heeled shoes, make her legs look even longer. Yet media advertising reinforces an image of Barbie being an ideal image of beauty. (Natenshon, 2004)

The average 3-10 year old girl in the United States owns eight Barbies. Only one percent of this group owns no Barbies. A 2006 study tested girls in grades kindergarten through second grade. Significantly, those who had seen Barbie had significantly more negative body satisfaction than those who hadn't. The researchers argued that the negative body image associated with Barbie may be an indication of body dissatisfaction, which can lead to depression and possible a precursor to eating disorders. (Dittmar, Halliwell, & Ive, 2006)

Girls also are exposed to other numerous artificial role models. Many cartoons feature impossibly thin females from Judy Jetson, Wilma Rubble, Veronica and Betty (from the Archie series) to the female characters in the Cartoon Network's Atomic Betty and Class of 3000. Disney features thin female characters such as Ariel, the Little Mermaid, and Jasmine from Aladdin, who show lots of cleavage. Of interesting note, Disney characters from long ago (such as Snow White) were of a more normal body size. (Lamb & Brown, 2006) MGM Entertainment engages young girls through an interactive web site YummiLand.com that targets four to ten year old girls. The web site features the

Soda Pop Girls, who though thin, interestingly interact on a cartoon web site with candy and malt shops and all seem to be eating away on empty calorie products with no ill effects. (Blank, 2006) Another recent cartoon, the Bratz Girls, feature a popular group of slim high school girls. The message is quickly evident – to be popular, girls must be thin. The Bratz Girls was turned into a movie featuring real characters in 2006, furthering their influence on young girls.

Studies show that children by the age of six to nine years old acquire an active dislike of the obese body and that by age seven they have assimilated adult cultural perceptions of attractiveness. (Feldman, Feldman, & Goodman, 1988) Another study found that girls as young as 12 years old placed greater emphasis on their body's appearance than on their competence. (Slater & Tiggermann, 2002) Given all the media images featuring thin body types, researchers have found girls as young as nine years old that show considerable dissatisfaction with their body shapes. (Hill, Draper, & Stack, 1994) Another survey found over half of adolescent girls wanted to be thinner. (Maloney, McGuire, Daniels, & Specker, 1989) Another study reported a significant proportion of girls within or even below their normal weight range were not comfortable with their size. (Moses, Banilivy, & Lifshitz, 1989)

Thin idealized bodies are used to persuade girls to purchase products and pursue strategies in order to change the appearance of their bodies. Numerous studies have detailed the great extent to which adolescent girls pursue coping strategies to deal with their insecurities with their bodies. Teenage girls 12 to 19 years of age spent over $8 billion on beauty products in 1997 – spending more in this product category than in any other except for clothing and jewelry. (Parks, 1998) Frequent exposure to cultural beauty ideals through the media has been linked with higher rates of eating disorders. Researchers have connected the incidence of anorexia nervosa (characterized by self-starvation and excessive weight loss) among 10 to 19 year old girls as fashion and body image changed over a 50 year period. The thin ideal proceeded the times when the rates of anorexia nervosa were highest. (Lucas, Beard, O'Fallon, & Kurland, 1991)

76

Adolescent girls seek out plastic surgery as an alternative to correct their perceived body deficiencies. Over 77,000 procedures were performed on teens 18 and younger in 2005, a 15% increase since 2000. (L.Zurbriggen, et al., 2007) Associations between body dissatisfaction and the onset of cigarette smoking among adolescent girls under the belief that smoking will enable them to control their weight and meet the standards of physical appearance considered desirable. (Camp, Klesges, & Relyea, 1993)

Marketing Body Image to Women

Older women feel the pressures of achieving a thin firm beauty ideal as well. A research study consisting of women ages 20 to 60 years old who were exposed to ads featuring thin models expressed more body-focused anxiety than those exposed to average size or no models. (Dittmar & Howard, Thin-ideal Internalization and Social Comparison Tendency as Moderators of Media Models' Impact on Women's Body-focused Anxiety, 2004) A study found that women overestimate the size of their hips by 16% and their waists by 25%. In a Glamour survey, 61% of respondents said they were ashamed of their hips, 64% were ashamed of their stomachs, and 72% were ashamed of their thighs. (The Media and Eating Disorders) Sales of anti-aging beauty products increased to over $11 billion worldwide. (Phillips, 2006) Cosmetic surgery is on the rise as consumers struggle for the perfect body, no matter what the costs to their health, lifestyle, or budgets. Data from the American Society of Plastic Surgeons show how the pressure to stay young and thin has affected American women. Between 2000 and 2005, surgeons performed a 115% increase in tummy tucks, a 283% increase in buttock lifts, a 3,413% increase in upper arm reductions and a 4,101% increase in lower body lift procedures. (American Society of Plastic Surgeons, 2006)

The exposure to thin models and actresses in marketing ads lead to a distorted body image that have been linked to negative outcomes such as chronic dieting. (Lavine, Sweeney, & Wagner, August, 1999) When asked about their life's fears, most women respond with the fear of gaining weight. The diet industry alone is worth an estimated $100 billion. (Beauty and Body Image in the Media) Chronic dieting often produces a cycle of weight loss, followed by weight gain. Repetitive, or yo-yo dieting, can lead to loss of bone mass and increase the risk of developing osteoporosis. (Dean, 2001)

Many women are dieting and fall into eating disorders that are detrimental to their health. Media and marketing images present an idealized shape which is invested with the attributes of being attractive, desirable, successful, and loveable but which is unattainable. In one study, 30% of women surveyed chose an ideal body shape that is 20% underweight while 44% chose an ideal shape that was 10% underweight. (Media and Eating Disorders) Media influences on body image harms females' self esteem and promotes the risk of developing an eating disorder as she turns to trying to control her body to feel loved, accepted, and respected. (Jade, 2002)

Models also fall under great pressures to become and stay slim. One model named Crystal tells a particularly chilling tale. When she was 14 years old, she thought her dreams had come true when a talent agent encouraged her to pursue a career as a fashion model. The agent mentioned one catch – Crystal would need to lose ten inches off her hips. At the time she was 5'9" tall and weighed 165 pounds. She started out with a healthy diet that helped her lose thirty pounds. But then she hit a plateau and moved to some extreme measures to drop more weight. She began exercising three hours a day, seven days a week. After two years of extreme dieting Crystal's weight fell to a dangerously thin 95 pounds. At this point her agent finally landed her a modeling contract. However, after six months of fashion shoots and runways, her body began breaking down. She refused to give up on her modeling dreams and eventually became one of the most successful plus size models ever. She states that she'd like to see the fashion industry adopt a more open approach to models' bodies: "They should have petite women, they should have thin women, they should have curvy women. So if I'm a young girl looking up at the runway, then I'm like, 'Well, my body type's up there and I'm fine.'" (Breaking the Mold, 2006)

The Image Industry

Women who are insecure about their bodies may be motivated by social and self-esteem fears (see Chapter 2) and therefore more likely to purchase beauty products, new clothes, and diet aids. Women spend $3 billion on cosmetics, $2 billion on hair products, and $800 million on feminine hygiene products each year. (Dean, 2001)

Interestingly, as technology becomes more sophisticated, the ability to create an idealized body shape artificially becomes relatively easy. Beautiful models are often promoted as natural looking. But everyone has flaws such as a blemish, a not quite perfect stomach, or perhaps breasts not quite large enough to meet the marketers' standards they wish to project. Retouching allows media images to do away with these imperfections while appearing realistic despite their heavy editing and refining. Digital retouching also intensifies the unrealistic goal of perfect beauty. This raises an ethical issue by itself: does digital manipulation to create a perfect unattainable vision of beauty create an impossible standard for female consumers to meet? Editors suggest that the use of digital imaging simply mimics reality. (Wheele & Gleason, 1995) Artists argue that digital manipulation reflects the freedom to express their aesthetics and values. (Betts, 2003) However, what responsibility should editors, technicians, and artists carry when considering the consequences of the images presented in a commercial setting? What role do media play in a society that relies on the information and visual images they see for their overall social health?

Theoretical Perspectives

Two alternatives psychologists put forward to describes the power of media are cognitive and social comparison theories. Readers may recall the theory of reasoned action (which incorporates both cognitive and social, or normative means to influence consumer attitudes) from chapter 2 as well. The ideal self image may be considered as either an internal ideal (cognitive) or a societal ideal, resulting from what society dictates is the perfect body.

Cognitive theories highlight the automatic and unconscious nature of schemas and other cognitive thoughts that occur as a consumer responds to a communication. Schema represents a set of associations linked to a concept. Schema may contain a variety of associations and work best when they are favorable and salient. Ultra-thin models constitute stimuli that are relevant to women's appearance schemata, and are likely to lead to appearance schema activation when they are exposed to them. When marketers create images of thin models as beautiful, sexy, and glamorous, women cannot help but feel dissatisfied with their body image, in essence producing a think thin and feel bad sequence. (Brown & Dittmar, 2005)

Social comparison theory proposes that individuals, when objective means of evaluating one's self are not available, are driven to compare themselves with other people, including those portrayed in ads. Dissatisfaction occurs when a discrepancy exists between the ideal state and the actual state. Females who are inundated with thin models presented as society's view of attractiveness perceive these models to be the norm for feminine beauty. One outcome of this comparison is that consumers do not feel adequate if they do not live up to the comparison person. (Richins, 1991) One researcher found that women not only compare themselves to others to evaluate their attractiveness, but also to the images presented to them in the mass media. The research further found that the effects of social comparison to idealized media images raised comparison standards for attractiveness and lowered satisfaction with one's own attractiveness. (Richins, Social Comparison and the Idealized Images of Advertising, 1991) Teens are particularly vulnerable. One study found that adolescents, characterized by pressures to be thin faced body dissatisfaction along with deficits in social supports, were adversely affected by exposure to these images.

Marketing Body Image to Males: The Adonis Complex

Men, and in particular, young males face a somewhat similar problem as women. Advertisers present the ideal, handsome, sexually attractive male today as pumped up, with muscular shoulders and arms that quickly taper to washboard abdominal muscles. This new male look in ads displays muscularity, athleticism, and often sport tight shirts, tank tops, or no shirt at all. Research appears to support that social comparison is a fairly powerful predictor of body-image investment among many adolescents. (Morrison, Kalin, & Morrison, 2004)

The trend for men to create an Adonis look appears to have more recently arisen than the issues faced by women described earlier in this chapter. A 1997 study found that 45% of American men were dissatisfied with their muscle tone, almost double found in the same survey conducted in 1972. More than half were dissatisfied with their abdomen (63%) or weight (52%). When considering the male stars of the past like Clark Gable, Jimmy Stewart, Gregory Peck, and Cary Grant to more recent stars such as Arnold Schwarzenegger, Sylvester Stallone, and Jean-Claude van Damme, one can quickly see how the male celebrity model has changed. Young men growing up today are subject to thousands of supermale images who are clearly linked to social, financial, and sexual success. Like the female models described previously, these models represent standards no man can measure up to successfully. (Pope, Phillips, & Olivardia, 2000)

The Adonis look is incorporated in males at a young age. Boys' action figures are setting unrealistic ideals for boys much in the same way that Barbie dolls create an unrealistic ideal of thinness for girls. Consider action figure toys with muscle bound professional wrestlers and characters like G.I. Joe and action superheroes like Batman and Superman who all demonstrate to young boys what an admired adult male could look like. Action figures have been shown to be more muscular today than in previous generations. A 1998 G.I. Joe was found to be more muscular than the 1973 version. Wolverine, an X-Men action figure, has a bicep measurement equal to his waist measurement and a chest that is twice the size of his waist; this type of muscularity is unrealistic and like Barbie's figure,

81

cannot be accomplished. (Bartlett, 2005) The fact that the male action toy market exceeds $1 billion in sales annually strongly suggests that the body image message conveyed by these action figures carries a great impact on boys. (Pope, Phillips, & Olivardia, 2000)

While women are afflicted by eating disorders such as anorexia nervosa, males may experience their own obsessive-compulsive disorders that may be triggered by all the media images they encounter. These men are obsessed with achieving an unrealistic standard of muscularity as masculinity. A male may see himself as scrawny and inadequate and pursue unhealthy behaviors to become muscular at the expense of family, relationships, and career. (Cortese, 2004)

As many as 10% of males pursue unhealthy behaviors to compensate for a perceived inadequate body. These numbers are on the rise and may even be underreported since males are often reluctant to acknowledge any illness. (Waxman, 1998) To help manage their weight, boys ages nine to fourteen who though they were overweight were 65% more likely to think about or try smoking than their peers. Boys who worked out every day in order to lose weight were twice as likely to experiment with tobacco. (Marcus, 1999) Even more alarming, anabolic steroids are increasingly used for the purpose of enhancing male physical appearance. Different classes of steroids have been found to injure the liver, be linked to body tumors, create the presence of abnormal sperm cells, decrease sperm production, and atrophy a man's testes. (Kuipers, 1998) As steroid abuse increases, so do reports of physical dependence, major mood disorders, and psychoses. (Neimark) Men may not only experience violent reactions while on steroids but also depressive reactions when coming off steroids. (Pope, Phillips, & Olivardia, 2000)

All these issues point to a mental disorder formally called muscle dysmorphia, or to a layman bigorexia, where men view themselves through a distorted lens and become fixated about what they perceive as their physical inadequacies. This condition is often underdiagnosed because for men, being big is acceptable. In a study of over 1,000 men, over 50% were unhappy with their bodies and 40% said they would consider chest implants to achieve bigger pectorals. When asked to draw their ideal body, men's body ideal was so muscular it could only be achieved by taking the risks associated with anabolic steroids.

Many men are impacted by their body insecurities in other ways. Men now spend billions on surgical cosmetic procedures in order to improve their appearance. American men spend over $2 billion annually on commercial gym memberships and a similar amount on home exercise equipment. The market for men's fitness magazines has surged. One particular publication, *Men's Health*, grew more than six fold over seven years Many health and exercise magazines from hard core body building to magazines aimed at weekend athletes have arisen. Although these magazines may have words like health and fitness in their titles, they are often heavily focused on body appearance. Many of these magazines didn't exist a generation ago. (Pope, Phillips, & Olivardia, 2000)

Further Consequences to This Issue

Women and men appear to be ready and willing to spend unnecessary large amounts of money and engage in risky unhealthy behaviors to achieve the cultural ideal body image. This ideal body, heavily promoted by mass media, is virtually impossible to attain. This issue is problematic as time, attention, and monetary resources steal from other activities and issues that might empower women rather than making them feel inadequate. While this chapter has been critical of marketers, media, the fashion industry, and all who employ unattainable body models in their advertising, one must also balance the perspective that their marketing technique was not intentionally meant to cause harm.

Exhibit 6-1 points out women's feelings about how the media portrays them. The average American woman weighs 144 pounds and wears between size 12 and 14. The average fashion model weighs 23% less than the average female. A woman between the ages of 18-34 has only a seven percent chance of being as slim and a one percent chance of being as thin as a supermodel. Women are becoming more outspoken of their desire to see beauty defined in a more reasonable manner. In fact, 59% of women say that beauty changes over time because beauty is connected to certain situations and life moments. (Etcoff, Orbach, Scott, & D'Agostino, 2004) Marketers need to be cognizant of those needs (indeed, is not marketing focused on recognizing consumer needs and responding to them?) and the fact that how they portray body image is unreasonable and can cause harmful effects to the very consumers they serve. Companies are starting to take note and respond accordingly. Companies need to consider supporting media literacy that helps people of all ages to become better educated regarding the advertising techniques used to influence them to purchase products or pursue a particular behavior. Media literacy can be directed through educational systems and possibly through the health system. Media education intervention allows consumers of all age groups to learn to critically evaluate program and advertising content. (Committee on Public Education, Media Education, 1999)

Exhibit 6-1

The Media and Beauty

I wish female beauty was portrayed in the media as being made up of more than just physic attractiveness.	85%
I wish the media did a better job of portraying women of diverse physical attractiveness – age, shape, and size.	80%

Source: "The Real Truth About Beauty: A Global Report"

The Marketing Industry Responds to Criticism

Exhibit 6-2 points out how women wish to be portrayed differently than the ultra-thin models used in advertising and on runways. As pressures mount, companies are considering change. Unfortunately, a tragedy came along to accelerate the change in cultural norms of beauty. Ana Carolina Reston, 21, was a Brazilian fashion model who worked in runways around the world. She also appeared in print ads, showing off the creations of top designers. Unfortunately her desire to stay thin turned into an eating disorder. She existed on apples and tomatoes, and her weight plummeted to 88 pounds (on a 5'8'' frame). Her body mass index (BMI) was 13.4, a classification described by the World Health Organization as dangerously thin. So dangerously thin that despite the best efforts of her doctors, she died. Hers was not the first superthin model's death due to an eating disorder. Companies around the world started to respond. Madrid Fashion Week banned models with a BMI lower than 18. Organizers of similar fashion events in Brazil and Argentina have done the same and fashion leaders in Milan, Italy plan to pursue a similar plan. Unfortunately most of the United States fashion industry to date has been reluctant to adopt similar measures. (The Skinny on Models, 2007) However, to its credit, the Council of Fashion Designers of America released recommendations that while not binding, establish guidelines for keeping models under 16 off fashion runways and educating those in the industry about eating disorders. (Weight Standards Recommended for NYC Fashion Models, 2007) The guidelines may be found in the appendix. Male fashion designers and modeling agencies are starting to follow suit. "Designers are clearly more conscious that their consumer is a very, very broad spectrum of male," says Sean Patterson, president of a modeling agency. So designers and agencies have started to shift to using a more natural, regular looking male model, who while looking fit, clearly are no longer beefy hunks. (Smith, 2007)

Exhibit 6-2

Better Ways to Depict Women in the Media

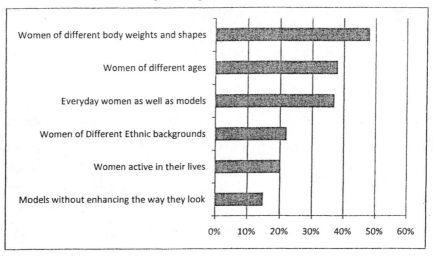

Source: The Real Truth About Beauty: A Global Report

Dove, a division of Unilever, commissioned a report to further understanding of women, beauty, and well-being. Dove's goals were concerned about the limited portrayal of women in the media and to explore what beauty means to the women and why that is. Further, Dove wanted to "assess whether it was possible to talk and think about female beauty in ways that were more authentic, satisfying, and empowering. Exhibit 6-3 highlights one component of the report's findings that provide a particularly critical review of women's perceptions of American media and advertising. (Etcoff, Orbach, Scott, & D'Agostino, 2004)

After reviewing the report's conclusions, Dove launched the "Campaign for Real Beauty" in September 2004. The ad campaign featured women whose appearances are outside the stereotypical norms of beauty as presented in the media. The Dove mission is to encourage women to feel more beautiful every day, to challenge the media's view of beauty, and to inspire women to take better care of their selves. The campaign is intended to serve as a starting point for societal change and act as a catalyst for widening the definition and discussion of beauty. (Real Women Bare Their Real curves, 2005) One of the means to substantiate Dove's campaign is to use real women in their ad campaigns, elevating ordinary women into honorary beauties. (Clegg, 2005) The campaign has seen mixed results. Dove experienced double digit sales increases during the first two years of the ad campaign. But Dove's sales are up only 1.2% so far in 2007. Possible the allure of the campaign is growing stale for Dove's consumers. (Neff, 2007)

Other companies are starting to follow along. Kellogg's Special K launched an ad campaign that encourages women not to obsess about their body image. Body shop, a chain of beauty and bath product stores, features Ruby, a plastic doll with a size 18 figure. (Goodman, 1998) Nike introduced a real women campaign that celebrates big butts, thunder thighs, and tomboy knees. The campaign features women sized six to twelve. While still below the average women's size, Nike's campaign represents a step away from the ultra thin models. (Sheppard, 2005)

In summary, marketers need to take responsibility for their part in creating the consumers' culture. They can do so by truly considering the needs of the women and men they target to serve. First, consider hiring models that present a greater range of body shapes. They can influence people, especially children and adolescents, from making weight an issue in their lives. Finally, consider assisting programs that provide educational assistance in media literacy in order to help people understand how advertising influences them. Hopefully, the marketing profession has turned the corner on this ethical issue and will continue to seek reforms on how advertisers present themselves to the public.

Exhibit 6-3

Popular Portrayals of Beauty/Physical Attractiveness

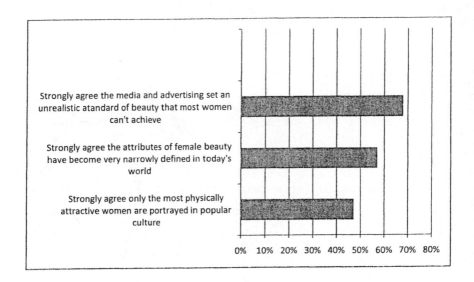

Source: The Real Truth About Beauty: A Global Report

Chapter 7

Losing Consumer Trust: The Trade-Off Between Consumer Privacy and Personalized Service

"There was of course no way of knowing whether you were being watched at any given moment. It was even conceivable that they watched everybody all the time. You had to live – did live, from habit that became instinct – in the assumption that every sound you made was overheard, and except in darkness, every movement scrutinized"

- *George Orwell*

George Orwell in the 21st Century

George Orwell incorporates in the plot of his novel "Nineteen Eight-Four", a look at how the protagonist in the story must deal with the government (also known as "Big Brother") monitoring everything he does and says. During the course of the novel, he manages to elude the government for a short while, but after he is caught, he pays a heavy price by being tortured and brainwashed. (Orwell, 1949) Americans today may not only be concerned about government monitoring their activities, but also businesses as well. Lest anyone think Orwell's view of the loss of privacy in the future to be pure fantasy, many instances of a big brother out there who sees and knows all does exist today. Consider the following story from the iMarketing News editor, Ken Magill:

"iMarketing News new e-mail services provider offers the ability to see who clicks on which articles in the DM News and iMarketing News e-mail newsletters. A colleague dropped by carrying a list of such e-mail addresses last week.

'Want to see who read your editorial this morning? He asked.

89

'What do you mean?'

'We can track who clicks on stories now,' he said. 'Here's a list of people's e-mail addresses who clicked on your editorial this morning. I just thought you might want to see it.'

He handed it over.

Scanning it immediately resulted in a minor, but persistent case of the creeps. People read in anonymity, or at least they believe they're reading in anonymity. Imagine the shock that could be delivered by simply sending an email like the following:

> 'Hey Bob@widgets.com, thanks for reading my editorial this morning! Frankly, Bob, I'm honored that you value it enough t read it with your Monday morning coffee. While I'm here, Bob, are there any topics you'd like to see addressed in the future?'

No, it's safe to assume that Bob would not like that kind of contact at all."
(Magill, 2002)

Before 2000, most consumers preferred to believe that the businesses who gather their information were trustworthy and kept this information private and confident. But technology also allows organizations to delve into consumers' personal lives to a greater extent than ever before thought possible. One car rental company used the global positioning system installed in their fleet of cars to track how their customers drove their vehicles. One customer found out that while he was using the rental his debit card was charged three times for speeding violations. The driver sued the rental company. Included in the court records were maps that showed the exact longitude and latitude of where he sped along with the exact second he was speeding, all provided from the tracking technology installed in the car. (Robert O'Hara, 2005)

Why Consumers Are Concerned

Various research studies and surveys reveal consumer unease:

- 70% say that companies have too much personal information. (Study: 70% of Customers Say Companies Know Too Much, 2003)
- A poll of 1,529 adults, found that 75% believe that their information will be shared without their permission and that 69% felt that hackers can steal their data. (Thibodeau, 2002)
- 76.4% felt that their privacy was compromised if a company uses the collected information to sell them products. (Study: 70% of Customers Say Companies Know Too Much, 2003)
- 80% of consumers stated they were very concerned or somewhat concerned about misuse of credit card data on the internet.
- 89% said that retailers are not doing everything they should to protect personal information. (Random Sampling: Talk to the Hand, 2004)
- Online spending would be 24% higher if not for privacy concerns. (Privacy Worries Plague E-Biz, 2002)
- 71% felt that protecting personal information and privacy is more of a concern now than a few years ago. (Random Sampling: Talk to the Hand, 2004)

Despite these concerns, consumers stated they were willing to relinquish personal information if the company offers a personalized product or service in return. (Study: 70% of Customers Say Companies Know Too Much, 2003) Exhibit 7-1 demonstrates that while consumers are apprehensive regarding the collecting of their confidential information, they also desire the marketing benefits that the use of this information brings.

A Marketing Perspective on Consumer Privacy

As technology becomes more sophisticated and prevalent, the ability for businesses to provide increasingly personalized attention to customers increases. Information can be gathered, stored, analyzed, and shared at incredible speeds. Richard Barton, a lawyer for the Direct Marketing Association, states "We have the capability to gather, store, analyze, segment and use for commercial purposes more data about people than was ever dreamed of. And technology is providing us with even more ingenious ways to reach into the lives of every American." (Robert O'Hara, 2005)

When used responsibly, consumers' personal information allows businesses to meet individuals' needs through customized service, rapid response to consumer requests, and rewarding loyal customers. Rapid check verifications and credit transactions have been made available from large, centralized databases. The compilation and analysis of consumer data allows businesses to use purchasing and demographic information to target customers more efficiently and effectively. Firms use confidential information to customize products and services. Consider a particular bar who serves approximately 10,000 people a week. In order to enter the bar and to check to see if the person is of legal drinking age, the customer must have their driver's license swiped through a data checking system. This system also collects each customer's name, address, and other personal details such as sex, height, eye color, and sometimes even social security numbers found embedded on a data strip on the back of the license. The bar owner tracks the information to build mailing lists and to track loyal customers. (Lee, 2002) New technology such as radio frequency identification (RFID) tags may be embedded in products and possibly allow organizations to track people's movement raises the specter of some form of a Big Brother never envisioned by George Orwell. (The Radio Age, 2006)

92

Exhibit 7-1

The Top Marketing Practices Desired By Consumers

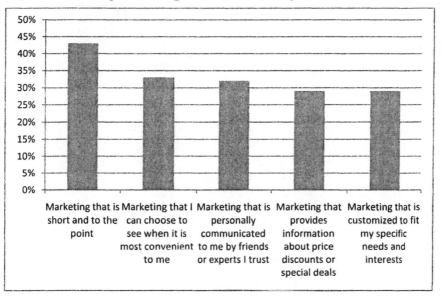

Source: Marketing News, December 15, 2005

Marketers V.S. Consumers: Ethical Concerns

Many people view privacy as a fundamental right while many corporations believe individual privacy does not exist. Not being concerned about privacy allows corporations to learn everything possible about their customers and therefore serve them better through customization and new commercial opportunities. The customer now becomes an object that accumulates commercial value. Businesses feel competitive pressures which in turn encourage them to seek new ways to reach new and current customers. Many companies collect and compile detailed financial and personal information without individual consent or knowledge (such as the bar owner in the previous paragraph). All this information, whether needed or not is stored in a database.

Issues arise as to how all the information is dealt with by the company. A poor data security system may allow the information to be stolen. Many companies don't track what information they're collecting or where it's kept. A company's marketing division may not communicate with the information technology division that they are gathering new types of records. Some companies may not realize the sensitive nature of the data they're collecting. Companies are drowning in data, much of it duplicative, and many simply don't have clear processes for dealing the integrity of their information or disposing of unneeded files. (Lewis, 2005)

Personal information has become a commercial commodity, available for sale or purchase to other organizations. Consumers' confidential information is available from list brokers, public databases, credit reporting agencies, and is shared among financial institutions, direct marketers, internet advertisers, and many others. What is becoming increasingly apparent is that consumer trust is being taken advantage of and in some cases abused. Responsible firms need to proactively balance how to ethically and legally employ consumer private information with legitimate concerns on how that information is used.

Nowhere are consumer privacy issues more evident than on the internet. Websites today are like sponges, soaking up all the information from each visitor they can. Websites can determine certain information about individuals through the use of cookies, spyware, or simply getting consumers to volunteer their information. Cookies and spyware are files and software placed on an individual's computer hard drive to monitor a user's activity, such as how they maneuver through the web site. These high tech tracking devices can also monitor a user's interest in up to 800 marketing categories including recency, frequency, and duration of the user's visit to a particular site. (Magill, 2002) Industry analysts estimate that 67% of all computers are infected by some form of spyware. Spyware infections prompted almost 1 million U.S. households to replace their computers in a six month period in 2006. Third party firms have stepped in to provide the technological means to gather data for companies.

94

These third parties deliver their own cookie files to a user's computer that tracks individual's clickstream patterns across different web sites. Many people, annoyed with all the companies trying to track them, obtained blocking software that block cookies and spyware. (Computer Spyware Course Earns 'A' in Outrage, Praise, 2006)

Consider companies such as Amazon.com, which has patented technology aimed at tracking information about their customers and on the people for whom its customers buy gifts. For years, Amazon has collected detailed information regarding what its customers buy, considered buying, browsed for, but never bought, recommended to others, or even wished someone would buy for them. Amazon uses that information to recommend more purchases, direct searches toward products it thinks you're most likely to want, or even stop the forgetful from buying a book they already may have purchased in the past. Amazon has also launched a web search engine called A9 that can remember everything that a consumer has searched for online. But privacy advocates are concerned because the site reserves the right to share that information with its retailing arm. Some privacy advocates believe Amazon is becoming close to emulating "Big Brother." Amazon sees such data gathering as the best way to keep their customers happy and loyal, a relationship building technique that they claim is crucial to competing. (Amazon.com Knows What You Bought - and Will Buy, 2006)

All the data collected by companies raise yet another concern. Poor security over databases, more sophisticated thieves, and the rising demand for identities has lead to data breaches and as a result identity theft. A 2003 Federal trade Commission survey showed that more than 27 million Americans have been victim of identity theft. (Robert O'Hara, 2005) People whose identities have been stolen can spend months or years along with thousands of dollars cleaning up the mess thieves have made with their good name and credit. Victims of identity theft may loose job opportunities, be refused loans, or even be arrested for crimes they didn't commit. Victims often feel humiliated, angry, and frustrated as they undertake the process to reclaim their identity. (ID Theft:

When Bad Things Happen To Your Good name, 2002)   Consumer fears of identity theft dramatically decreases their trust to purchase from an online retailer they haven't done business with in the past. A 2007 survey conducted by a data-loss-prevention services provider and a privacy and information-management research firm revealed that 36% of respondents would not use their credit or debit cards with a web merchant they didn't know. Another survey stated that 54% of consumers believe identity theft and fraud to be their biggest financial concerns. (Campanelli, 2007)

A Legal Perspective of Privacy

Personal privacy represents an important component of American culture. The U.S. Constitution, state constitutions, federal laws and regulations, and state statutes all address personal privacy to varying degrees. The typical privacy perspective attempts to balance the user's need to know the information with the degree of intrusion on the subject's reasonable expectation of privacy. Key federal legislation includes:

- The Privacy Act of 1974 which created a code of fair information practices regarding the collection, maintenance, use, and dissemination of personal information by the federal government. (Overview of the Privacy Act of 1974, 2004 Edition, 2004)
- The Children's Online Privacy Protection Act (COPPA) of 1998 prohibits operators of web sites or other online services directed to children from collecting personal information from children under the age of 13 without parental permission.
- The Fair and Accurate Credit Transactions Act of 2003 (FACTA) limits the ability of affiliated companies to use shared consumer data for marketing purposes.
- The CAN-SPAM Act of 2003 specifies email controls to attempt to limit junk email activity. Civil penalties of $250 per violation

with a cap of $2 million may be assessed to those who do not comply with this law.

- Several financial and credit reporting laws pertaining to handling consumer data and addressing identity theft issues were passed in 2003. The Internet Spyware Prevention Act, or I-SPY, which would allow for fines and prison terms for those who placed unauthorized code on a computer and use it to obtain or transmit personal information. (Dilworth D. , Anti-Spyware Bill Passed, 2007)

As data breaches escalate both federal and state governments have stepped in to attempt to address consumers' concerns. In 2005, President Bush established an identity-theft task force composed of federal agencies and led by the Federal Trade Commission and the Department of Justice. The report focused on four main areas. First, the report addresses the need to keep sensitive consumer data out of the hands of thieves through better data security and education. Second, the task force wants want to make to increase the difficulty for identity thieves who obtain consumer data to use it to steal identities. A third point the force addressed is assisting the victims of identity theft in recovering from the crime. The last goal is to deter identity theft through more aggressive prosecution and punishment of those who commit identity theft crimes. (Gellman, 2006)

When government has been slow to step in, private parties have taken matters into their own hands by suing companies for violating various existing federal laws. A group of cable subscribers initiated a class action suit that brought claims that Time Warner had failed to provide adequate notice that the cable company was selling subscribers' personal information to third parties and improperly disclosed subscribers' programming selections to third parties without offering subscribers a valid opt-out method. The suit alleged violations of both state consumer protection laws and the Cable Communications Policy Act of

1984. In another particular heinous example of identity theft, a woman was stalked and murdered after the perpetrator purchased personal information about her from the operators of an internet based information services firm. The New Hampshire Supreme Court ruled that an information broker selling personal information to a client has a legal duty to the person to which that information pertains, especially true when the investigator does not know the client or the client's purpose in seeking the information. The court found that obtaining and selling an individual's social security number without the individual's knowledge or permission is liable for damages. (Stephen Ambrose & Gelb, 2004)

How Should Privacy Concerns Be Addressed?

Americans are behind many other countries regarding how they treat an individual's privacy. The European Union has forged ahead in dealing with privacy issues. The EU has already implemented laws that grant consumers the right of full access to any and all information that companies maintain on them. (Barrett, 2002) Another EU privacy guideline suggest that companies aim to provide short, condensed privacy notices in their literature. This more easily understandable format will allow consumers to compare privacy notices of one company with other companies.

Database information generates direct economic benefits for consumers. Research has shown that property financing costs in the United States are approximately two percent less than in countries with restrictive data policies, translating into thousands of dollars of savings for every homeowner. Another study by the Information Services Executive Council and the Direct Marketing Association found that consumers would pay an additional $1 billion for the same apparel products if consumer information had not been readily available. This same study found that the cost of doing business under more stringent privacy laws would increase by 3.5 to 11 percent, which could drive smaller firms out of business. (Barrett, 2002)

So how should business manage consumer and government concerns while strategizing to utilize consumer information to more effectively compete? Interestingly enough, a 1973 government report entitled "Code of Fair Information Practices" provides the ethical foundation for companies to respect an individual's privacy:

- No secret data record-keeping systems should exist.
- People must be given the opportunity to find out what information is recorded about them and how it is used.
- People must be given the opportunity to prevent personal information from being used other than what it was originally collected for.
- People must be given the opportunity to correct records containing information about them.
- Organizations that create and use personal records must assure the reliability of the data and take precautions to prevent its misuse. (Severson, 1997)

Along a similar vein, the Federal Trade Commission (FTC) has outlined a set of principles for web sites that collect consumer information. Elements of those guidelines provide a foundation for legally and ethically gathering, using, and disposing consumers' confidential information:

- A notice should be published that is clear and conspicuous about what information is collected, how it is collected and used, and whether the information is disclosed to other entities.
- Consumers should be provided with a choice as to how their personal information may be used beyond the immediate transaction.

- Consumers should be granted access to personal information collected and have a reasonable opportunity to correct any errors.
- Companies should ensure they offer consumers security that their information will be protected. (Burgunder, 2007)

One alternative means for a company to publicly demonstrate their information standards is to work through third party organizations that have a stake in privacy issues by creating certification programs that state standards of information privacy. One such certifier, TRUSTe, a nonprofit organization founded in the mid 1990's, created a "trustmark" to firms that meet its privacy principles and pledge to cooperate with resolving consumer complaints. TRUSTe regularly follows up with web sites to ensure the companies are complying with their guidelines. TRUSTe has also developed an online consumer grievance mediation process. (Burgunder, 2007)

In order to provide consumers a choice in how their information may be used, companies must be proactive and move beyond the data collecting and mining systems used over the last few years. Too often privacy issues are left to the purview of an organization's Information Technology (IT) department. Unfortunately, the IT department may not communicate effectively with the marketing department (and vice versa). The complex legal and ethical intricacies of managing consumer information may call for the creation of a privacy department. At the very least a company privacy representative may be needed. This person should be directly involved with writing an organization's privacy statement. A privacy statement should be written as clearly and succinctly as possible to allow consumers to truly understand how the company they're dealing with will handle their information. The head of privacy concerns in any organization needs to review what information the company is collecting, how that information is secured, who has access to that information, how is the information used, and what third parties, if any, is this information transferred to. (Chapell, 2006)

Consumers want control over their information. About 73% of Americans appear to be sensitive about their privacy. Consumers are more willing to share more of their personal information and do more business with companies they trust. (Giordano, 2007) They want companies that gather their data to use fair practices that are clearly outlined to them. They are often willing to share pertinent data to allow a better customized experience. Many consumers don't want their information shared and want the company to ask their consent before sharing their confidential information with a third party. When garnering consent, consider the issues outlined in chapter 3 to asking consumers for their permission. Permission marketing unleashed tremendous synergies between company and consumer that benefits both parties. These policies will also work toward establishing the trust that consumers desire and will allow organizations to build a better relationship with their customers. Interestingly, people who care most about privacy see real value in receiving tailored marketing content.

Chapter 8

"My Brand is the Best!" - Puffery and Deceptive Advertising Practices

"Oh, what a tangled web we weave, when first we practice to deceive!"

- *Sir Walter Scott*

Puffery Defined

You are now reading the greatest marketing ethics book ever written. While this statement may sounds impressive, the final judgment lies in the reader's mind! Puffery is most commonly known as the exaggerated commendation for promotional purposes. (Merriam-Webster Online Dictionar, 2006) Puffery represents the advertiser's opinion and often employs subjective, superlative terms in describing the qualities of a product or service. Often this claim is so exaggerated as to be obviously untrue. (Hoffman, 2006) Consider the following real life marketing slogans sampled from one Sunday newspaper:

- "Your perfect look is at your fingertips…"
- "Get vibrant hair that makes everyone else blush"
- "It flexes to closely fit your curves revealing smooth skin worthy of a goddess."
- "Helps your child master the bathroom."
- "The world's finest artificial Christmas trees"
- "New advanced portable heater can cut your heating bill up to 50%"
- "Own the vehicles that own the road"

103

Many companies walk a fine line by embellishing their product's attributes. Two researchers exposed 100 subjects to five advertisements containing 13 puffing claims. Interestingly, 80.5% of the time the subjects saw the ads to be making puffing claims. The researchers also noted that the subjects believed the explicit puffing claims in 39.6% of the instances where they had the opportunity to see them conveyed. (Rotfeld & Rotzoll, 1981)

Puffery vs. Deceptive Advertising

For marketing to be effective, consumers must have confidence that the company is acting in a forthright manner. However, puffing should not be confused with deceptive advertising. Any kind of deception discourages a consumer's trust and is ultimately, self defeating and may be considered illegal.

The United States government regulators have found that while puffs are false, they are not deceptive. Federal laws assume that most consumers will act reasonably by distrusting puffery and therefore not be deceived or hurt by it. The Federal Trade Commission (FTC), the government agency that oversees advertising, has long held that deception exists when an objectively ascertainable material fact is presented falsely, is ambiguous, or is misleading. The FTC standard deals with the number of consumers who need to be affected by the advertising for deception to exist, the consumer's intelligence and knowledge, and that the belief formed from the ad is factually untrue or misleading. (Gardner, 1975) The FTC hasn't provided any more specific guidelines and all disputes are handled on a case by case basis. Two particular examples point to the difference between puffery and deceptive advertising. McDonald's sells a product that they call a "Quarter-Pounder." But that is not how much the burger weighs after it is cooked. The FTC found that most people understood that hamburgers shrink when cooking and that McDonald's wasn't trying to purposely deceive anyone. In a different vein, Klondike advertised that their ice cream bars were "93% Fat Free Frozen Dessert with chocolate-flavored coating." The FTC found that while the bars were only 93% fat free if the consumer picked off the layer of chocolate and that Klondike was deceiving the public with their claim. (Gourley, 1999)

So how does a company distinguish whether their advertising claims are deceptive or not? FTC Commissioner Roscoe B. Starek, III, addressed what distinguishes deceptive advertising from puffery by preparing a listing of common myths about advertising claims:

1. Myth #1 – A claim can be substantiated if it has several studies supporting it. Truth: A claim can only be substantiated if the studies were scientifically controlled and support the claim in the view of experts in the field and the party conducting the study had no incentive to obtain particular results. A claim may be substantiated if there is an absence of relevant studies contradicting the results.

   An unsubstantiated claim may arise if other studies contradict or raise questions about the study findings, the study has a design flaw(s) or was conducted by persons with an incentive to obtain particular results.

2. Myth #2 – If your product has some benefit, the advertisement will not be challenged. Truth: Even real product claims must be substantiated with scientific evidence.

3. Myth #3 – Testimonials are substantiation. Truth: Testimonials are not considered to be substantiation for a claim, even if testimonials are backed up with affidavits from individual users stating the product performed as promised. The FTC does not consider anecdotal evidence (i.e., testimonials) sufficient to support a claim. An endorser should be an expert in the area for which he is acting

as a spokesperson and their message should be based on evaluation or tests other experts in the field would find sufficient to support the expert endorser's statements.

4. Myth #4 – If endorsers actually use and like the product, it is safe to use their endorsements. Truth: Given that the endorser uses and is making truthful statements about the product, the claim must consider whether the results the endorser experienced are typical. If the results are not substantiated, then the claim needs to be qualified by a clear and prominent disclosure of the generally expected results for users of the product (i.e., results may not be typical).

5. Myth #5 – If a deceptive claim is followed with a disclosure, liability is removed. Truth: If a claim cannot be substantiated do not make it. The claim may have to be narrowed down to what can be substantiated. Disclosures that flatly contradict a deceptive claim, or purport not to make a claim does not remove liability.

6. Myth #6 – The use of a "results may vary" statement is adequate to remove liability. Truth: Even while the disclosure is very prominent and obvious, it does not keep consumers from believing that these results are typical of what they can expect from using the product. Therefore, there is liability.

The conclusion drawn from these myths is that objective claims must be substantiated while subjective claims are generally considered puffery and cannot be substantiated. (Starek, 1996)

To Puff Or Not To Puff?

Why use hype to puff a product? Advertisements need to stand out to create consumer awareness. Puffing can be used to grab a consumer's attention, often in an entertaining way. A recent battery commercial shows how the Energizer Bunny steps in when a power utility company experiences a crisis and manages to keep a city lit. While no consumer believes that batteries have the power needed to keep a city lit, the humorous message gets across the point that this brand sells powerful batteries. Many marketers believe that puffing encourages consumers to view their product in a more favorable light and therefore reach a positive attitude toward the product and brand.

Ivan Preston, a Journal Communications Professor of Advertising at the University of Wisconsin Madison, ranks puffery into six categories as described in Exhibit 8-1. The claims at the top of the list are most likely to be false and deceptive because they have no factual basis for their claim. The ones at the bottom of the list are most subjective and therefore less deceptive in nature. These puffing categories often consist of weasel words that are used to make claims about a product sound like proven facts. For example, Bounty has long advertised their paper towels as the "Quicker-picker-upper." This form of puffery comes across as an incomplete comparison that makes Bounty sound like they are the best paper towel in the industry. The prerequisite question is "Quicker than what?" Without any factual comparisons, there is nothing to prove as fact. Another form of weasel words can take the form of a hollow phrase. The beef industry used once used a slogan "Beef - real food for real people." So all other foods must be artificial? Note how the use of weasel words adds glamour to an ordinary product. (Weasel Words, 1999)

Exhibit 8-1

The 6 Categories of Puffery

"Best"	• "Nestle's makes the very best chocolate" • "Nobody gets the dirt out like Hoover"	Expresses uniqueness or that no competitor is as good.
"Best possible"	• "Perfect rice everytime" (Minute Rice) • "Nothing cleans stains like Clorox Bleach"	While best means better than all others, this category allows some others to be as good, though none are better.
"Better"	• "Advil just works better" • "For dazzling, whiter teeth" (Aquafresh)	This means better than at least some of the competitors' products. Although others could be equal or better. It might imply being the best.
"Specially good"	• If it's Weber, it's great outdoors." • "Extraordinary elegance" (Coty)	These products place high but do not explicitly call themselves best or better.
"Good"	• "M'm M'm good." (Campbell's Soup) • "We bring good things to life" (General Electric)	They show favorableness without any explicit terms.
"Subjective qualities"	• "There's a smile in every Hershey's Bar" • "Taste the future" (Budweiser Ice Draft)	These products make no explicit claims, but imply one. This category is most oriented to subjectivity, sometimes fancifully unreal.

Source: "Puffery and Other 'Loophole' Claims: How the Law's 'Don't Ask, Don't Tell' Policy Condones Fraudulent Falsity in Advertising" by Ivan L. Preston

Legal Repercussions

Puffery implies potential legal issues. Product claims that are factually false or convey a false impression have the power to deceive or mislead reasonable people. Puffery can serve as a form of legal defense to a charge of misleading consumers or that the company has made a legal cognizable promise.

In essence, companies apply puffery when sued on charges of false advertising or in a failure to meet a product's warranty provisions. (Hoffman, 2006)

The National Advertising Review Council (NARC), established in 1971 by various marketing and advertising organizations, promotes and enforces standards of truth, accuracy, taste, morality, and social responsibility in advertising. Because NARC operates quickly, informally, and at a modest cost, it is perceived as more beneficial to resolve advertising disputes than through the court system. The NARC encompasses the National Advertising Division (NAD). The NAD monitors advertising practices and reviews complaints about advertising from consumers, consumer groups, competitors, Better Business Bureau, trade associations and other interested parties. When the NAD fields a valid complaint, it contacts the advertiser, specifying any claims to be substantiated. If the NAD finds the substantiation inadequate, it request modification or discontinuance of the claims. If the NAD and an advertiser reach an impasse, either party has the right to a binding review by a five member panel. If an advertiser refuses to comply with the panel's decision, the dispute is referred to an appropriate government body. Interestingly, no party has yet ever disputed a panel's decision, an argument for self-regulation. (Arens, 2005)

Puffery is often perceived as contradictory. As Ivan Preston says advertisers defend puffery

"... because it's legal, but it can only be legal if it doesn't work. If consumers reject puffery as the advertisers claim, there is no reason to use it. They would be defending it for a reason that tells them there's no point in defending it. A sensible reason for using false puffery could only be that it works, which would then make it illegal." (Preston, 1996)

One of the downsides of puffing a product is that consumers start to become more skeptical of a company's claims. As consumers become savvier in their evaluation of advertising, consumers are likely to become more discerning regarding the credibility of the ad's assertion. Marketers may wish to determine how believable consumers perceive their claims and to measure how consumer's belief levels regarding puffed claims are affecting sales of their products.

Chapter 9

Marketing Ethics - Conclusions

"Never let your sense of morals prevent you from doing what is right!"

Isaac Asimov

Marketing represents the most visible business activity. Advertising continually risks criticism by inviting consumers to try their products and services. A company's reputation is on the line if their offering does not meet with their promise as communicated through marketing. Marketing has an extensive influence on the American economy and culture. Marketing communications can serve to educate and entertain. By associating products with a desirable image, advertising offers people the opportunity to satisfy psychological or emotional needs. Marketing encourages completion that is especially evident through new and improved products that are introduced to the market. New and differentiated products provide more choice to consumers.

However, the marketing profession's excess and wastefulness has led many critics and consumer advocates to harshly stating that advertising is evil and extends too much control over people. A common belief that has been a reoccurring theme in this book is that marketing can be manipulative and deceptive. Some critics believe advertising manufactures consumer demand for products they might not otherwise feel a need to buy. One particular detractor commented that "Advertising is the science of arresting the human intelligence long enough to get money from it." (Hood, 2006)

Many of the advertising issues addressed in the previous chapters suggests that advertising projects false stereotypical images, such as presenting waif thin models as glamorous and sexy or that living in a McMansion is the only way to

111

demonstrate your success to the world. These images can make people feel uncomfortable, vulnerable, and moved to fit in with society by making them feel unhappy with their self esteem, talents, and personality. Because marketing encourages people to purchase what they may not need, Americans have incurred high levels of debt to buy items that contribute to waste, pollute, and cause harm to the environment. Marketers can be accused of presenting false messages to manipulate people through fear appeals, puffery, or targeting a marketing campaign to children disguised as an educational program. Marketing absorbs a great deal of time and resources that are passed along to consumers as a business expense. The resources expended ultimately add more product costs that show up in higher prices. Marketers are accused of invading people's privacy to blatantly sell consumer's information as a means to generate extra revenues.

Marketers respond to these accusations by stating that advertising allows a company to make higher level of sales which in turn reduces the per product cost which in turn keeps prices down. Marketers believe that they provide information that allows consumers to arrive at an effective purchase decision. Advertising has been said to encourage people to work towards a better life. Marketers advocate that their profession increases competition which causes companies to continually seek improvement in product development and customer service. The profession will state that marketing merely reflects rather than instigates American culture and societal values. Finally, many marketing professionals argue that ultimately, consumers have free will to choose to allow how (if at all) advertising to influence their lives.

The reality is, of course, somewhere between the critics' position and the defensive stance by the marketing profession. Marketing does indeed reflect the American culture and values, but also takes part in determining cultural values through their advertising decisions. Using idealistic unattainable models creates a norm of how people are expected to look, even if the attempt to reach that norm is pursued through unhealthy life choices. Marketing may exert too much influence over consumers' lives. The market research profession continually examines psychological and emotional means to influence people's behaviors. Most people are not educated regarding these approaches. Certainly most troubling is how some companies manipulate the most innocent of all, young children.

The ethical issues described in this book pervade American culture today. Ethical marketing involves actions that the marketer and its peers believe is morally right in a given situation. The marketing profession is responsible for exercising honesty and integrity in their relationships while adhering to professional ethical standards. Ultimately, the marketing industry has been given a great deal of latitude and managed to avoid the institution of strict regulation in the United States. While the industry is to be commended to attempt to self-regulate, most consumers today continue to cynically view advertising as manipulative. Companies will need to reconsider the ethical implications of their decisions and act before government steps in. The American Marketing Association Code of Ethics represents a solid foundation to start. The marketing industry must consider more specific standards that address the special issues outlined in this book. As can be seen from the current privacy legislation proposals, failure to do so may result in legal solutions being imposed on ethical issues – a possibility that no one in the marketing field wants.

American Marketing Association
Code of Ethics

ETHICAL NORMS AND VALUES FOR MARKETERS

Preamble

The American Marketing Association commits itself to promoting the highest standard of professional ethical norms and values for its members. Norms are established standards of conduct that are expected and maintained by society and/or professional organizations. Values represent the collective conception of what people find desirable, important and morally proper. Values serve as the criteria for evaluating the actions of others. Marketing practitioners must recognize that they not only serve their enterprises but also act as stewards of society in creating, facilitating and executing the efficient and effective transactions that are part of the greater economy. In this role, marketers should embrace the highest ethical *norms* of practicing professionals and the ethical *values* implied by their responsibility toward stakeholders (e.g., customers, employees, investors, channel members, regulators and the host community).

General Norms

1. Marketers must do no harm. This means doing work for which they are appropriately trained or experienced so that they can actively add value to their organizations and customers. It also means adhering to all applicable

laws and regulations and embodying high ethical standards in the choices they make.

2. Marketers must foster trust in the marketing system. This means that products are appropriate for their intended and promoted uses. It requires that marketing communications about goods and services are not intentionally deceptive or misleading. It suggests building relationships that provide for the equitable adjustment and/or redress of customer grievances. It implies striving for good faith and fair dealing so as to contribute toward the efficacy of the exchange process.

3. Marketers must embrace, communicate and practice the fundamental ethical values that will improve consumer confidence in the integrity of the marketing exchange system. These basic *values* are intentionally aspirational and include honesty, responsibility, fairness, respect, openness and citizenship.

Ethical Values

Honesty- to be truthful and forthright in our dealings with customers and stakeholders.

- We will tell the truth in all situations and at all times.
- We will offer products of value that do what we claim in our communications.
- We will stand behind our products if they fail to deliver their claimed benefits.
- We will honor our explicit and implicit commitments and promises.

Responsibility- to accept the consequences of our marketing decisions and strategies.

- We will make strenuous efforts to serve the needs of our customers.
- We will avoid using coercion with all stakeholders.
- We will acknowledge the social obligations to stakeholders that come with increased

  marketing and economic power.
- We will recognize our special commitments to economically vulnerable segments of the   market such as children, the elderly and others who may be substantially disadvantaged.
- Fairness- to try to balance justly the needs of the buyer with the interests of the seller.
- We will represent our products in a clear way in selling, advertising and other forms of communication; this includes the avoidance of false, misleading and deceptive promotion.
- We will reject manipulations and sales tactics that harm customer trust.
- Wc will not engage in price fixing, predatory pricing, price gouging or "bait-and-switch" tactics.
- We will not knowingly participate in material conflicts of interest.

Respect - to acknowledge the basic human dignity of all stakeholders.

- We will value individual differences even as we avoid stereotyping customers or depicting demographic groups (e.g., gender, race, sexual orientation) in a negative or dehumanizing way in our promotions.
- We will listen to the needs of our customers and make all reasonable efforts to monitor and improve their satisfaction on an ongoing basis.
- We will make a special effort to understand suppliers, intermediaries and distributors from other cultures.
- We will appropriately acknowledge the contributions of others, such as consultants, employees and coworkers, to our marketing endeavors.

Openness- t o create transparency in our marketing operations.

- We will strive to communicate clearly with all our constituencies.
- We will accept constructive criticism from our customers and other stakeholders.
- We will explain significant product or service risks, component substitutions or other foreseeable eventualities that could affect customers or their perception of the purchase decision.
- We will fully disclose list prices and terms of financing as well as available price deals and adjustments.

Citizenship- to fulfill the economic, legal, philanthropic and societal responsibilities that serve stakeholders in a strategic manner.

- We will strive to protect the natural environment in the execution of marketing campaigns.
- We will give back to the community through volunteerism and charitable donations.
- We will work to contribute to the overall betterment of marketing and its reputation.
- We will encourage supply chain members to ensure that trade is fair for all participants, including producers in developing countries.

Implementation

Finally, we recognize that every industry sector and *marketing subdiscipline (e.g.,* marketing *research,* e-commerce, *direct selling, direct marketing, advertising)* has its own specific ethical issues that require policies and commentary. An array of such codes can be accessed through links *on the AMA Web* site. We encourage all such groups to develop and/or refine their industry and *discipline-specific* codes of ethics to supplement these general norms and values.

PARENTS' BILL OF RIGHTS

WHEREAS, the nurturing of character and strong values in children is one of the most important functions of any society;

WHEREAS, the primary responsibility for the upbringing of children resides in their parents;

WHEREAS, an aggressive commercial culture has invaded the relationship between parents and children, and has impeded the ability of parents to guide the upbringing of their own children;

WHEREAS, corporate marketers have sought increasingly to bypass parents, and speak directly to children in order to tempt them with the most sophisticated tools that advertising executives, market researchers and psychologists can devise;

WHEREAS, these marketers tend to glorify materialism, addiction, hedonism, violence and anti-social behavior, all of which are abhorrent to most parents;

WHEREAS, parents find themselves locked in constant battle with this pervasive influence, and are hard pressed to keep the commercial culture and its degraded values out of their children's lives;
WHEREAS, the aim of this corporate marketing is to turn children into agents of corporations in the home, so that they will nag their parents for the things they see advertised, thus sowing strife, stress and misery in the family;

WHEREAS, the products advertised generally are ones parents themselves would not choose for their children: violent and sexually suggestive entertainment, video games, alcohol, tobacco, gambling and junk food;

WHEREAS, this aggressive commercial influence has contributed to an epidemic of marketing-related diseases in children, such as obesity, type 2 diabetes, alcoholism, anorexia and bulimia, while millions will eventually die from the marketing of tobacco;

WHEREAS, corporations have latched onto the schools and compulsory school laws as a way to bypass parents and market their products and values to a captive audience of impressionable and trusting children;

WHEREAS, these corporations ultimately are creatures of state law, and it is intolerable that they should use the rights and powers so granted for the purpose of undermining the authority of parents in these ways;

119

THEREFORE, BE IT RESOLVED, that the U.S. Congress and the fifty state legislatures should right the balance between parents and corporations and restore to parents some measure of control over the commercial influences on their children, by enacting this Parents' Bill of Rights, including:

Leave Children Alone Act. This act bans television advertising aimed at children under 12 years of age. (federal)

Child Privacy Act. This act restores to parents the ability to safeguard the privacy of their own children. It gives parents the right to control any commercial use of personal information concerning their children, and the right to know precisely how such information is used. (federal, state)

Advertising to Children Accountability Act. This act helps parents affix individual responsibility for attempts to subject their children to commercial influence. It requires corporations to disclose who created each of their advertisements, and who did the market research for each ad directed at children under 12 years of age. (federal)

Commercial-Free Schools Act. Corporations have turned the public schools into advertising free-fire zones. This act prohibits corporations from using the schools and compulsory school laws to bypass parents and pitch their products to impressionable schoolchildren. (federal, state)

Fairness Doctrine for Parents. This act provides parents with the opportunity to talk back to the media and the advertisers, It makes the Fairness Doctrine apply to all advertising to children under 12 years of age, providing parents and community with response time on broadcast TV and radio for advertising to children. (federal)

Product Placement Disclosure Act. This law gives parents more information with which to monitor the influences that prey upon their children through the media. Specifically, it requires corporations to disclose, on packaging and at the outset, any and all product placements on television and videos, and in movies, video games and books. This prevents advertisers from sneaking ads into media that parents assume to be ad-free. (federal)

Child Harm Disclosure Act. Parents have a right to know of any significant health effects of products they might purchase for their children. This act creates a legal duty for corporations to publicly disclose all information suggesting that their product(s) could substantially harm the health of children, (federal)

Children's Food Labeling Act. Parents have a right to information about the food that corporations push upon their children. This act requires fast food restaurant chains to label contents of food, and provide basic nutritional information about it. (federal, state)

Children's Advertising subsidy Revocation Act. It is intolerable that the federal government actually rewards corporations with a big tax write-off for the money they spend on psychologists, market researchers, ad agencies, media and the like in their campaigns to instill their values in our children. This act eliminates all federal subsidies, deductions and preferences for advertising aimed at children under 12 years of age. (federal)

CARU's Core Principles

The following Core Principles apply to all practices covered by the self-regulatory program.

1. Advertisers have special responsibilities when advertising to children or collecting data from children online. They should take into account the limited knowledge, experience, sophistication and maturity of the audience to which the message is directed. They should recognize that younger children have a limited capacity to evaluate the credibility of information, may not understand the persuasive intent of advertising, and may not even understand that they are being subject to advertising.

2. Advertising should be neither deceptive nor unfair, as these terms are applied under the Federal Trade Commission Act, to the children to whom it is directed.

3. Advertisers should have adequate substantiation for objective advertising claims, as those claims are reasonably interpreted by the children to whom they are directed.

4. Advertising should not stimulate children's unreasonable expectations about product quality or performance.

5. Products and content inappropriate for children should not be advertised directly to them.

6. Advertisers should avoid social stereotyping and appeals to prejudice, and are encouraged to incorporate minority and other groups in advertisements and to present positive role models whenever possible.

7. Advertisers are encouraged to capitalize on the potential of advertising to serve an educational role and influence positive personal qualities and behaviors in children, e.g., being honest, and respectful of others, taking safety precautions, engaging in physical activity.

8. Although there are many influences that affect a child's personal and social development, it remains the prime responsibility of the parents to provide guidance for children. Advertisers should contribute to this parent-child relationship in a constructive manner.

122

D.   Guidelines

1. An Overview

The Core Principles are broad in scope and reflect the belief that responsible advertising comes in many forms and that diversity should be encouraged. They aim to cover the myriad advertising practices in today's marketplace, as well as those that may emerge as technologies and advertising practices evolve. The Guidelines below are designed to provide additional guidance to assist advertisers in applying these broad principles to their child-directed advertising and to help them deal sensitively and honestly with children.

The Guidelines are not intended to be exhaustive. With respect to advertising practices that are not specifically addressed, CARU will apply the above Core Principles in evaluating the practices.

Part I of the Guidelines offers general guidance on deception and other marketing practices that are inappropriate when directed to children, and encourages certain practices. Part II addresses online data collection and other privacy-related practices that pose special concerns for children and require more specific guidance.

2.   **Part I: General Guidelines**

(a)   **Deception**

To assure that advertising directed to children is not deceptive:

1.   The net impression" of the entire advertisement, considering, among other things, the express and implied claims, any material omissions, and the overall format, must not be misleading to the children to whom it is directed.

2.   Whether an advertisement leaves a misleading impression should

be determined by assessing how reasonable children in the intended audience would interpret the message, taking into account their level of experience, sophistication, and maturity; limits on their cognitive abilities; and their ability to evaluate the advertising claims.

(b)   Product Presentations and Claims

To avoid deceptive and/or inappropriate advertising to children involving product presentations and claims:

1. Copy, sound and visual presentations should not mislead children about product or performance characteristics. Such characteristics may include, but are not limited to, speed, method of operation, color, sound, durability, nutritional benefits and similar characteristics.

2. The presentation should not mislead children about benefits from use of the product. Such benefits may include, but are not limited to, the acquisition of strength, status, popularity, growth, proficiency and intelligence.

3. Claims should not unduly exploit a child's imagination. While fantasy, using techniques such as animation and computer-generated imagery, is appropriate for both younger and older children, it should not create unattainable performance expectations nor exploit the younger child's difficulty in distinguishing between the real and the fanciful.

4. Advertisements should demonstrate the performance and use of a product in a way that can be duplicated by a child for whom the product is intended.

5. The advertisement should not mislead children about what is included in the initial purchase.

6. Advertising that compares the advertised product to another product should be based on real product attributes and be understandable to the child audience.

7. The amount of product featured should not be excessive or more than would be reasonable to acquire, use or consume by a person in the situation depicted. For example, if an advertisement

124

depicts food being consumed by a person in the advertisement, or suggests that the food will be consumed, the quantity of food shown should not exceed the labeled serving size on the Nutrition Facts panel; where no such serving size is applicable, the quantity of food shown should not exceed a single serving size that would be appropriate for consumption by a person of the age depicted.

8.   Advertising of food products should encourage responsible use of the product with a view toward healthy development of the child. For example, advertising of food products should not discourage or disparage healthy lifestyle choices or the consumption of fruits or vegetables, or other foods recommended for increased consumption by current USDA Dietary Guidelines for Americans and My Pyramid, as applicable to children under 12.

9.   Advertisements for food products should clearly depict or describe the appropriate role of the product within the framework of the eating occasion depicted.

     a.   Advertisements representing a mealtime should depict the food product within the framework of a nutritionally balanced meal.

     b.   Snack foods should be clearly depicted as such, and not as substitutes for meals.

(c)   Material Disclosures and Disclaimers

1.   All disclosures and disclaimers material to children should be understandable to the children in the intended audience, taking into account their limited vocabularies and level of language skills. For young audiences, simple words should be chosen, *e.g.,* "You have to put it together." Since children rely more on information presented in pictures than in words, demonstrative disclosures are encouraged.

2.   These disclosures should be conspicuous in the advertising format and media used, e.g., online, advertisers should make disclosures clear and proximate to, and in the same format (i.e., audio or graphic) as, the claims to which they are related; in television, advertisers should use audio disclosures, unless disclosures in other formats are likely to be seen and understood by the intended audience.

3.　Circumstances where material disclosures are needed include, but are not limited to, the following:

    a.　Advertising for unassembled products should clearly indicate they need to be put together to be used properly.

    b.　If any item essential to use of the product is not included, such as batteries, this fact should be disclosed clearly.

    c.　Advertisers should clearly disclose information about products purchased separately, such as accessories or individual items in a collection.

    d.　If television advertising to children involves the use of a toll-free telephone number, it must be clearly stated, in both audio and video disclosures, that the child must get an adult's permission to call. In print or online advertising, this disclosure must be clearly and prominently displayed.

4.　Advertisers that create or sponsor an area in cyberspace, either through an online service or a Website, must prominently identify the name of the sponsoring company and/or brand in that area. This could be done by using wording such as "Sponsored by _____ "

5.　If videotapes, CD-ROMS, DVDs or software marketed to children contain advertising or promotions (e.g., trailers) this fact should be clearly disclosed on the packaging.

(d)　Endorsements

1.　Advertisers should recognize that the mere appearance of a celebrity or authority figure with a product can significantly alter a child's perception of the product. Advertisers may use such personalities as product endorsers, presenters, or testifiers, but they must take great care to avoid creating any false impression that the use of the product enhanced the celebrity's or authority figure's performance.

2.　All personal endorsements should reflect the actual experiences and beliefs of the endorser.

3.　An endorser who is represented, either directly or indirectly, as an expert must possess qualifications appropriate to the particular expertise depicted in the endorsement.

(e)   Blurring of Advertising and Editorial/Program Content

1.   Advertisers should recognize that children may have difficulty distinguishing between program/editorial content and advertising, e.g., when program /editorial characters make advertising presentations or when an advertisement appears to be content to the intended audience.

2.   Advertising should not be presented in a manner that blurs the distinction between advertising and program/editorial content in ways that would be misleading to children.

3.   Prohibited practices in television advertising

      a.   Program personalities, live or animated, should not be used to advertise products, premiums or services in or adjacent to a television program primarily directed to children under 12 years of age in which the same personality or character appears.

      b..   Products derived from or associated with a television program primarily directed to children under 12 years of age should not be advertised during or adjacent to that program.

4.   In media other than television, a character or personality associated with the editorial/content of the media should not be used to sell products, premiums or services in close proximity to the program/editorial content, unless the advertiser makes it clear, in a manner that will be easily understood by the intended audience, that it is an advertisement.

5.   On Websites directed to children, if an advertiser integrates an advertisement into the content of a game or activity, then the

advertiser should make clear, in a manner that will be easily understood by the intended audience, that it is an advertisement.

6. If videotapes, CD-ROMS, DVDs or software marketed to children contain advertising or promotions (e.g., trailers), the advertising itself should be separated from the program and clearly designated as advertising.

(I)   Premiums, Kids' Clubs, Sweepstakes and Contests

1. Advertisers should recognize that their use of premiums, kids' clubs, contests and sweepstakes has the potential to enhance the appeal of their products to children.

2. Advertisers should take special care in using these kinds of promotions to guard against exploiting children's immaturity.

3. <u>Premiums</u>

   a. Since children have difficulty distinguishing product from premium, advertising that contains a premium message should focus the child's attention primarily on the product and make the premium message clearly secondary.

   b. Conditions of a premium offer should be stated simply and clearly.

4. Kids' Clubs

   a. Advertising should not mislead children into thinking they are joining a club when they are merely making a purchase or receiving a premium.

   b. Before an advertiser uses the word "club,"

certain minimum requirements should be met. These are:

5. Interactivity - The child should perform some act demonstrating an intent to join the club, and receive something in return. Merely watching a television program or eating in a particular restaurant, for example, does not constitute membership in a club.

6. Continuity - There should be an ongoing relationship between the club and the child member, e.g., a regular newsletter or activities scheduled over a period of time.

7. Exclusivity - The activities or benefits derived from membership in the club should be exclusive to its members, and not merely the result of purchasing a particular product.

   a. Additional requirements applying to kids' clubs online are covered in Part II of the Guidelines.

8. Sweepstakes and Contests

   a. Advertisers should recognize that children may have unrealistic expectations about the chances of winning a sweepstakes or contest or inflated expectations of the prize(s) to be won.

   b. The prize(s) should be clearly depicted.

   c. The free means of entry should be clearly disclosed.

   d. The likelihood of winning should be clearly disclosed in language readily understandable to the child audience. Disclosures such as, "Many will enter, a few will win." should be used, where appropriate.

   e. All prizes should be appropriate to the child audience.

f   Online contests or sweepstakes should not require the child to provide more information than is reasonably necessary. Any information collection must meet the requirements of the Data Collection section of the Guidelines and the federal Children's Online Privacy Protection Act (COPPA). For examples of compliant information collection practices for this purpose, please visit www.caru.org/news/commentary.asp.

(g)   Online Sales

1. Advertisers who sell products and services to children online should clearly indicate to the children when they are being targeted for a sale.

2. If an advertiser offers the opportunity to purchase any product or service, either through the use of a "click here to order" button or other on-screen means, the ordering instructions must clearly and prominently state that a child must have a parent's permission to order.

3. Online advertisers must make reasonable efforts, in light of all available technologies, to provide the person responsible for paying for such products and services the means to exercise control over the transaction.'

4. If no reasonable means is provided to avoid unauthorized purchases by children online, the advertiser should enable the person responsible for payment to cancel the order and receive full credit without incurring any charges.

(h)   Sales Pressure

1. Advertising should not urge children to ask parents or others to buy products. It should not suggest that a parent or adult who purchases a product or service for a child is better, more intelligent or more generous than one who does not.

2. Advertisers should avoid using sales pressure in advertising to children, e.g., creating a sense of urgency by using words

130

such as "buy it now."

3.   Advertisements should not convey to children that possession of a product will result in greater acceptance by peers or that lack of a product will result in less acceptance by peers.

4.   Advertisements should not imply that purchase or use of a product will confer upon the user the prestige, skills or other special qualities of characters appearing in advertising.

5.   Advertisements should not minimize the price of goods and services with words such as, "only," "just," or "bargain price" that children do not understand to be exaggeration or "puffing."

(i)   Unsafe Safety and Inappropriate Advertising to Children

1.   Guidelines

     a.   Advertisers should take into account that children are prone to exploration, imitation, and experimentation and may imitate product demonstrations or other activities depicted in advertisements without regard to risk.

     b.   Advertisers should not advertise products directly to children that pose safety risks to them, i.e., drugs and dietary supplements, alcohol, products labeled, "Keep out of the reach of children;" nor should advertisers targeting children display or knowingly link to pages of Websites that advertise such products.

     c.   Advertisements for children's products should show them being used by children in the appropriate age range. For instance, young children should not be shown playing with toys safe only for older children.

---

3 Requiring the use of a credit card in connection with a transaction is a reasonable effort to provide the person responsible for payment with control over the transaction. This is consistent with COPPA regulations. *See* 16 CFR § 312.5.

a. Advertisements should not portray adults or children in unsafe situations or in acts harmful to themselves or others. For example, when activities (such as bicycle riding or skateboarding) are shown, proper precautions and safety equipment should be depicted; when an activity would be unsafe without adult supervision, supervision should be depicted.

b. Advertisers should be aware that many childhood injuries occur from the misuse of common household products and should avoid demonstrations that may encourage inappropriate use of such products by children.

2.　　Inappropriate Advertising

a. Advertisers should take care to assure that only age appropriate videos, films and interactive software are advertised to children, and if an industry rating system applies to the product, the rating label is prominently displayed.[4]

b. Advertising should not portray or encourage behavior inappropriate for children (e.g., violence or sexuality) or include material that could unduly frighten or provoke anxiety in children; nor should advertisers targeting children display or knowingly link to pages of a Website that portray such behaviors or materials.

---

4 Violations of this guideline may be brought to the attention of the relevant rating entity.

3. Part II: Guidelines for Online Privacy Protection

This Part addresses concerns about the collection of personal data from children and other privacy-related practices on the Internet. Its provisions are consistent with the Children's Online Privacy Protection Act of 1998 (COPPA) and the FTC's implementing Rule, which protect children under the age of 13.

Online data collection from children poses special concerns. The medium offers unique opportunities to interact with children and to gather information for marketing purposes. Young children however, may not understand the nature of the information being sought or its intended uses, and the medium makes it easy to collect such data directly from children without the supervision or permission of their parents or guardians. The solicitation of personally identifiable information from children (e.g., full names, addresses, email addresses, phone numbers) therefore triggers special privacy and security concerns.

The guidelines below address those concerns by providing guidance on specific issues involving online data collection and other privacy-related practices by Website operators that target children under 13 years of age or that know or should know that a visitor is a child under 13 years of age.

(a) Data Collection

1. In collecting information from children under 13 years of age, advertisers should adhere to the following guidelines: Advertisers must clearly disclose all information collection and tracking practices, all information uses, and the means for correcting or removing the information. These disclosures should be prominent and readily accessible before any information is collected. For instance, on a Website where there is passive tracking, the notice should be on the page where the child enters the site. A heading such as "Privacy," "Our Privacy Policy," or similar designation is acceptable if it allows an adult to click on the heading to obtain additional information on the site's practices concerning information collection, tracking and uses.

2. Advertisers should disclose, in language easily understood by a child, (a) why the information is being requested (e.g., "We'll use your name and email to enter you in this contest and also add it to our mailing list") and (b) whether the information is intended to be shared, sold or distributed outside of the collecting company.

3. Advertisers should disclose any passive means of collecting information from children (e.g., navigational tracking tools, browser files, etc.) and what information is being collected.

4.   Advertisers must obtain prior "verifiable parental consent"[5] when they collect personal information (such as email addresses, screen names associated with other personal information, phone numbers or addresses) that will be publicly posted, thereby enabling others to communicate directly with the child online or offline, or when the child will be otherwise able to communicate directly with others.

5.   For activities that involve public posting, advertisers should encourage children not to use their full names or screen names that correspond with their email address, but choose an alias (e.g., "Bookworm," "Skater," etc.) or use first name, nickname, initials, etc.

6.   Advertisers should not require a child to disclose more personal information than is reasonably necessary to participate in the online activity (e.g., play a game, enter a contest, etc.).

7.   Advertisers must obtain prior "verifiable parental consent" when they plan to share or distribute personal information to third parties, except parties that are agents or affiliates of the advertiser or provide support for the internal operation of the Website and that have agreed not to disclose or use the information for any other purpose.

8.   When an advertiser collects personal information only for its internal use and there is no disclosure of the information, the company must obtain parental consent, and may do so through the use of email, coupled with some additional steps to provide assurance that the person providing the consent is the parent.

---

5 The definition of "verifiable parental consent" in the Children's Online Privacy Protection Rule applies. See 16 CFR § 312.5.

9.	When an advertiser collects and retains online contact information to be able to respond directly more than once to a child's specific request (such as an email newsletter or contest) but will not use the information for any other purpose, the advertiser must directly notify the parent of the nature and intended uses of the information collected, and permit access to the information sufficient to allow a parent to remove or correct the information.

10.	To respect the privacy of parents, advertisers should not maintain in retrievable form information collected and used for the sole purpose of obtaining verifiable parental consent or providing notice to parents, if consent is not obtained after a reasonable time.

11.	If an advertiser communicates with a child by email, there should be an opportunity with each mailing for the child or parent to choose by return email or hyperlink to discontinue receiving mailings.

### (b)	Age-Screening/Hyperlinks

1.	On Websites where there is a reasonable expectation that a significant number of children will be visiting, advertisers should employ age-screening mechanisms to determine whether verifiable parental consent or notice and opt-out is necessitated under the Data Collection provisions above.

2.	Advertisers should ask screening questions in a neutral manner so as to discourage inaccurate answers from children trying to avoid parental permission requirements.

3.	Age-screening mechanisms should be used in conjunction with technology, e.g., a session cookie, to help prevent underage children from going back and changing their age to circumvent age-screening.

4.	Since hyperlinks can allow a child to move seamlessly from one site to another, operators of Websites for children or children's portions of general audience sites should not knowingly link to pages of other sites that do not comply with CARU's Guidelines.

J. Women and the Media

234.   During the past decade, advances in information technology have
        facilitated a global communications network and transcends national
        boundaries and has an impact on public policy, private attitudes and
        behavior, especially for children and young adults. Everywhere the
        potential exists for the media to make a far greater contribution to the
        advancement of women.

235.   More women are involved in careers in the communications sector, but
        few have attained positions at the decision-making level or serve on
        governing boards and bodies that influence media policy. The lack of
        gender sensitivity in the media is evidenced by the failure to eliminate the
        gender-based stereotyping that can be found in public and private local,
        national and international media organizations.

236.   The continued projection of negative and degrading images of women in
        media communications- electronic, print, visual, and audio- must be
        changed. Print and electronic media in most countries do not provide a
        balanced picture of women's diverse lives and contribution to society in a
        changing world. In addition, violent and degrading or pornographic media
        products are also negatively affecting women and their participation in
        society. Programming that reinforces women's traditional roles can be
        equally limiting. The world-wide trend towards consumerism has created
        a climate in which advertisements and commercial messages often portray
        women primarily as consumers and target girls and women of all ages
        inappropriately.

237.   Women should be empowered by enhancing their skills, knowledge and
        access to information technology. This will strengthen their ability to
        combat negative portrayals of women internationally and to challenge
        instances of abuse of the power of an increasingly important industry.
        Self-regulatory mechanisms for the media need to be created and
        strengthened and approached developed to eliminated gender-biased
        programming. Most women, especially in developing countries, are not
        able to access effectively the expanding electronic information highways
        and therefore cannot establish networks that will provide them with
        alternative sources of information. Women therefore need to be involved
        in decisions-making regarding the development of the new technologies in

order to participate fully in their growth and impact.

238.   In addressing the issue of the mobilization of the media, Governments and other actors should promote an active and visible policy of mainstreaming a gender perspective on policies and programs.

Strategic objective J.1.

Increase the participation and access of women to expression and decision-making in and through the media and new technologies of communication

Actions to be taken

239.   By Governments:

   a.   Support women's education, training and employment to promote and ensure women's equal access to all areas and levels of the media;
   b.   Support research into all aspects of women and the media so as to define areas needing attention and action and reviewing existing media policies with a view to integrating a gender perspective;
   c.   Promote women's full and equal participation in the media, including management, programming, education , training and research;
   d.   Aim at gender balance in the appointment of women and men to all advisory, management, regulator or monitoring bodies, including those connected to the private and state or public media;
   e.   Encourage, to the extent consistent with freedom of expression, these bodies to increase the number of programs for and by women to see to it that women's needs and concerns are properly addressed;
   f.   Encourage and recognize women's media networks, including electronic networks and other new technologies of communication, as a means for the dissemination of information and the exchange of views, including at the international level, and support women's groups active in all media work and systems of communications to that end;
   g.   Encourage and provide the means or incentives for the creative use of programs in the national media for the dissemination of information on various cultural forms of indigenous people and the development of social and education issues in this regard within the framework of national law;
   h.   Guarantee the freedom of the media and its subsequent protection within the framework of national law and encourage, consistent with freedom of

expression, the positive involvement of the media in development and social issues.

240. By National and international media systems:

Develop, consistent with freedom of expression, regulatory mechanisms, including voluntary ones, that promote balanced and diverse portrayals of women by the media and international communication systems and that promote increased participation by women and men in production and decision-making.

241. By Governments, as appropriate, or national machinery for the advancement of women:

   a. Encourage the development of educational and training programmes for women in order to produce information for the mass media, including funding of experimental efforts, and the use of the new technologies of communication, cybernetics space and satellite, whether public or private;
   b. Encourage the use of communication systems, including new technologies, as a means of strengthening women's participation in democratic processes;
   c. Facilitate the compilation of a directory of women media experts;
   d. Encourage the participation of women in the development of professional guidelines and codes of conduct or other appropriate self-regulatory mechanisms to promote balanced and non-stereotyped portrayals of women by the media.

242. By non-governmental organizations and media professional associations:

   a. Encourage the establishment of media watch groups that can monitor the media and consult with the media to ensure that women's needs and concerns are properly reflected;
   b. Train women to make greater use of information technology for communication and the media, including at the international level;
   c. Create networks among and develop information programmes for non-governmental organizations, women's organizations and professional media organizations in order to recognize the specific needs of women in the media, and facilitate the increased

participation of women in communication, in particular at the international level, in support of South-South and North-South dialogue among and between these organizations, inter alia, to promote the human rights of women and equality between women and men;

d. Encourage the media industry and education and media training institutions to develop, in appropriate languages, traditional, indigenous and other ethnic forms of media, such as story-telling, drama, poetry and song, reflecting their cultures, and utilize these forms of communication to disseminate information on development and social issues.

Actions to be taken

243. By Governments and international organizations, to the extent with freedom of expression:

   a. Promote research and implementation of a strategy of information, education and communication aimed at promoting a balanced portrayal of women and girls and their multiple roles;
   b. Encourage the media and advertising agencies to develop specific programmes to raise awareness of the Platform for Action;
   c. Encourage gender-sensitive training for media professionals, including media owners and managers, to encourage the creation and use of non-stereotyped, balanced and diverse images of women in the media;
   d. Encourage the media to refrain from presenting women as inferior beings and exploiting them as sexual objects and commodities, rather than presenting them as creative human beings, key actors and contributors to and beneficiaries of the process of development;
   e. Promote the concept that the sexist stereotypes displayed in the media are gender discriminatory, degrading in nature and offensive;
   f. Take effective measures or institute such measures, including appropriate legislation against pornography and the projection of violence against women and children in the media.

244. By the mass media and advertising organizations:

   a. Develop, consistent with freedom of expression, professional guidelines and codes of conduct and other forms of self-regulation to promote the presentation of non-stereotyped images of women;

    b.   Establish, consistent with freedom of expression, professional guidelines and codes of conduct that address violent, degrading or pornographic materials concerning women in the media, including advertising;

    c.   Develop a gender perspective on all issues of concern to communities, consumers and civil society;

    d.   Increase women's participation in decision-making at all levels of the media.

245.   By the media, non-governmental organizations and the private sector, in collaboration, as appropriate, with national machinery for the advancement of women:

    a.   Promote the equal sharing of family responsibilities through media campaigns that emphasize gender equality and non-stereotyped gender roles of women and men within the family and that disseminate information aimed at eliminating spousal and child abuse and all forms of violence against women, including domestic violence;

    b.   Produce and/or disseminate media materials on women leaders, inter alia, as leaders who bring to their positions of leadership many different life experiences, including but not limited to their experiences in balancing work and family responsibilities, as mothers, as professionals, as managers and as entrepreneurs, to provide role models, particularly to young women;

    c.   Promote extensive campaigns, making use of public and private educational programmes, to disseminate information about and increase awareness of the human rights of women;

    d.   Support the development of and finance, as appropriate, alternative media and the use of all means of communication to disseminate information to and about women and their concerns;

    e.   Develop approaches and train experts to apply gender analysis with regard to media programmes.

Council of Fashion Designers of America Health Initiative

January 12, 2007 – New York – The **CFDA** recently formed a health initiative to address what has become a global fashion issue: the overwhelming concern about whether some models are unhealthily thin, and whether or not to impose restrictions in such cases. Designers share a responsibility to protect women, and very young girls in particular, with in the business, sending the message that beauty is health. While some models are naturally tall and thin and their appearance is a result of many factors including genetics, youth, nutritional food, and exercise, other models have or develop eating disorders. Although we cannot fully assume responsibility for an issue that is as complex as easting disorders and that occurs in many walks of life. The fashion industry can begin a campaign of awareness and create an atmosphere that supports the well-being of these young women. Working in partnership with the fashion industry, medical experts, nutritionists, and fitness trainers, the **CFDA** has formed a committee to propose a series of positive steps and are committed to industry-specific educational efforts, awareness programs, support systems, and evaluation and treatment options that advance our recommendations.

Recommendations:

- Educate the industry to identify the early warning signs in an individual at risk of developing an eating disorder.
- Models who are identified as having an eating disorder should be required to seek professional help in order to continue modeling. And models who are receiving professional help for an eating disorder should not continue modeling with out that professional's approval.
- Developing worships for the industry (including models and their families) on the nature of eating disorders, how they arise, how we identify and treat them, and complications if they are untreated.
- Support the well-being of younger individuals by not hiring models under the age of sixteen for runway shows; not allowing models under the age of eighteen to work past midnight at fittings or shoots; and providing regular breaks and rest.
- Supply healthy meals, snacks, and water backstage and at shoots and provide nutrition and fitness education.
- Promote a healthy backstage environment by raising the awareness of the impact of smoking and tobacco-related disease among women, ensuring a

142

smoke-free environment, and address underage drinking by prohibiting alcohol.

The **CFDA Health Initiative** is about awareness and education, not policing. Therefore, the committee is not recommending that models get a doctor's physical examination to assess their health or body-mass index to be permitted to work. Eating disorders are emotional disorders that have psychological, behavioral, social and physical manifestations, of which body weight is only one.

The **CFDA Health Initiative** is committed to the notion of a healthy mind in a healthy body, and there cannot be one with out the other. The industry is determined to foster a balanced approach to nutrition, recreation, exercise, work, and relationships. In support of our recommendations, the **CFDA** will present a discussion on health and beauty during Fashion Week on February 5 to an audience composed of designers, models, agents, editors, and industry leaders, along with representatives from eating-disorder organizations, nutritionist, and other health professionals.

Works Cited

(2005). *2005 Marketing Receptivity Survey.* Yankelovich Partners, Inc.

6 Strategies Marketers Use to Get Kids to Want Stuff Bad. (2006, November 22). *USA Today* , p. 01B.

About Book It. (2007, July 7). Retrieved July 7, 2007, from Bookitprogram.com: http://bookitprogram.com/parents/about.asp

About the Program. (2007, July 8). Retrieved July 8, 2007, from labelsforeducation.com: http://www.labelsforeducation.com/about.aspx

Abramovich, G. (2007, January 26). *Worlddata: E-mail Lists Continue CPM Slide.* Retrieved January 26, 2007, from dmnews.com: http://www.dmnews.com/cms/dm-news/list-services/39806.html

Acuff, D. S. (1997). *What Kids Buy and Why.* New York: The Free Press.

Ad Narcissicism, Ad Nauseum. (2002, December 9). *Marketing News* , p. 3.

'Advergames' Target Tween Market. (2005, January 30). *St. Cloud Times* , p. 1E.

AMA Updates Association's Code of Ethics. (2004, September 1). *Marketing News* , p. 40.

Amazon.com Knows What You Bought - and Will Buy. (2006, March 2). *St. Cloud Times* .

American Society of Pastic Surgeons. (2006). Retrieved September 8, 2006, from plasticsurgery.org: http://www.plasticsurgery.org/public_education/loader.cfm?url=/commonspot/security/getfile.cfm&PageID=17870

Americans Lack Money Cushion. (2007, February 2). *St. Cloud Times* , p. 1A.

Arens, W. F. (2005). *Contemporary Advertising 10th edition.* Columbus: McGraw Hill.

Arthur, D., & Queste, P. (2003). The Ethicality of Using Fear for Social Advertising. *Australasian Marketing Journal* , 12-27.

Bagdikian, B. H. (2000). *The Media Monopoly, Sixth Edition.* Beacon Press.

Barber, B. R. (2007). *Consumed: How Marketers Corrupt Children, Infantilize*

145

Adults, and Swallow Citizens Whole. New York: W. W. Norton & Company.

Barnouw, E. (1970). *A History of Broadcasting in the United States Vol. 3.* New York: Oxford University Press.

Barrett, J. (2002, July). Customer Data Integration Technology: A Privacy Solution. *The Computer & Internet Lawyer* , pp. 8-11.

Bartlett, C. (2005). *Action Figures and Men.* Retrieved April 24, 2007, from findarticles.com: http://findarticles.com/p/articles/mi_m2294/is_11-12_53/ai_n16083986/print

Beattie, J. (2002, August 22). *Stealth marketing Effective, Some Say Deceiving.* Retrieved September 7, 2007, from abcnews.com: http://abcnews.go.com/print?id=130164

Beauty and Body Image in the Media. (n.d.). Retrieved April 24, 2006, from www.media-awareness.ca: http://www.media-awareness.ca/english/issues/stereotyping/women_and_girls/women_bea...

Behind the Scenes: Hollywood Goes Hypercommercial (2000). [Motion Picture].

Bennett, J. (2006, August 18). *American Debt: Escaping the Credit Card Quagmire.* Retrieved September 3, 2007, from MSNBC.com: http://www.msnbc.com/id/14366431/site/newsweek/print/1/displaymode/1098/

Bennett, J. (2006, August 8). *Q & A: Why Consumer Debt is Rising.* Retrieved September 3, 2007, from MSNBC.com: http://www.msnbc.com/id/14521360/site/newsweek/print/1/displaymode/1098

Betts, K. (2003, February 2). The Man Who Makes the Pictures Perfect. *New York Times* , pp. Section 9, pp 1,8.

Blank, C. (2006, April 3). Yummi Promotion Sends Girls Online, to Stores. *DM News* , p. 4.

Breaking the Mold. (2006, November 7). Retrieved November 8, 2006, from oprah.com: http://www2.oprah.com/tows/slide/200611/20061107/slide_20061107_284_301.j html

Brody, J. (2005, January 31). Children, Media, and Sex: A Big Book of Blank Pages. *New York Times* .

Broome, E. C. (1929). *Report of the Committee on Propaganda in the Schools.* Atlanta: National Education Association.

Brown, A., & Dittmar, H. (2005). Think "Thin" and Feel Bad: The Role of Appearance Schema Activation, Attention Level, and Thin-Ideal Internalization for Young Women's Responses to Ultra-Thin Media Ideals. *Journal of Social and CLinical Psychology* , 8, 1088-1113.

Burgunder, L. (2007). *Legal Aspects of Managing Technology, 4th ed.* Thompson West Publishing: Eagen, Minnesota.

Camp, D., Klesges, R., & Relyea, G. (1993). The Relationship Betwen Body Weight Concerns and Adolescent Smoking. *Health Psychology* , pp. 12, 24-32.

Campanelli, M. (2007, July 23). Online Shoppers' Worries Over ID Teft Grow. *DM News* , p. 3.

Captive Kids: A Report on Commercial Pressures on Kids at School. (1990). Retrieved July 9, 2007, from consumersunion.org: http://www.consumersunion.org/other/captivekids/recommendations.htm

Carr, A. Z. (1968, January-February). Is Business Bluffing Ethical? *Harvard Business Review* , p. 46.

Carroll, A. B. (1989). *Business and Society: Ethics and Stakeholder Management.* Cincinnati, OH: South-Western.

Chafkin, M. (2006, May). School Ties. *Inc* .

Chapell, A. (2006, January 23). *Online Exclusive: Consumers Atill Aren't Careful Enough With Their Persoanl Information.* Retrieved January 23, 2006, from www.dmnews.com: http://www.dmnews.com/cgi-bin/artprevbot.cgi?article_id=35400

Chatzky, J. S. (2003, April 4-6). Parties Without the Presents. *USA Weekend* , p. 24.

Chatzky, J. S. (2003, April 4-6). Parties Without the Presents. *USA Weekend* , p. 24.

Clegg, A. (2005, April 18). *Dove Gets Real.* Retrieved April 27, 2006, from www.brandchannel.com: http://www.brandchannel.com/print_page.asp?ar_id=259&section=main

Cohen, M. J., Comrove, A., & Hoffner, B. (2005). The New Politics of Consumption: Promoting Sustainability in the American Marketplace. *Sustainability, Science, Practice, & Policy* , 58-74.

Cohn, L. D., & Addler, N. (1992). Female and Male Perceptions of Ideal Body Shapes. *Psycholgy of Women Quarterly* , 16, 69-79.

(1999). *Committee on Public Education, Media Education.* American Academy of Pediatrics.

Computer Spyware Course Earns 'A' in Outrage, Praise. (2006, November 2). *St. Cloud Times* , p. 6A.

Conaboy, R. P. (1995). Corporate Crime in America: Strengthening the Good Citizen Corporation. *U.S. Sentencing Commission* , pp. 1-2.

Cortese, A. J. (2004). *Provocateur: Images of Women anf Minorities in Advertising.* Lanham, Maryland: Rowman & Littlefield Publishers, Inc.

Counts, C. E. (2006, October 1). Interactivism Allows Consumers to Co-create, Grows Loyalty. *Marketing News* , p. 30.

Cover Concepts. (2007, July 12). Retrieved July 12, 2007, from Cover Concepts: http://www.coverconcepts.com

Credit Card Debt Consumer Crisis Looms . (2007, August 31). Retrieved September 3, 2007, from thestate.com: http://www.thestate.com/business/v-print/story/159751.html

Dalmeny, K. (2003, January/February). Food Marketing: The Role of Advertising in Child Health. *Consumer Policy Review* , pp. 2-7.

Danziger, P. (2002). *Why People Buy Things They Don't Need.* Ithaca, New York: Paramount Market Publishing, Inc.

Dean, A. (2001). *Body Images: Do You Hate Your Body?* Retrieved April 25, 2006, from U of A HealthInfo Site: http://www.uofaweb.ualberta.ca/CMS/printpage.cfm?ID=27650

Desjardin, J., & McCall, J. J. (2005). *Contemporary Issues in Business Ethics Fifth Edition.* Belmont, CA: Thomson Wadsworth.

Dilworth, D. (2007, May 7). Anti-Spyware Bill Passed. *DM News* , p. 1.

Dilworth, D. (2006, October 9). Family Grocer Gets Friendly Response From Mobile Offers. *DM News* , p. 8.

Dilworth, D. (2006, October 2). Restaurants Serve Sizzling E-mails. *DM News* , p. 21.

Dittmar, H., & Howard, S. (2004). Thin-ideal Internalization and Social

Comparison Tendency as Moderators of Media Models' Impact on Women's Body-focused Anxiety. *Journal of Social and Clinical Psychology* , pp. 23, 768-791.

Dittmar, H., Halliwell, H., & Ive, S. (2006). Does Barbie Make Girls Want to be Thin? . *Development Psychology* , pp. 42 (2) pp. 283-292.

Dumont, P. (2001, Semptember). *Temptation-free television for children?* Retrieved March 1, 2006, from The Courier UNESCO: http://www.unesco.org/courier/2001_09/uk/medias.htm

Durning, A. T. (1993, January/February). Long on Things, Short on Time. *Sierra* .

Eating Disorders: Body Imaging and Advertising. (n.d.). Retrieved March 24, 2006, from HealthyPlace.com: http://www.healthyplace.com/communities/Eating_Disorders/body_image_advert ising_.asp

Edwards, J. (2006, January 30). The Fine Line Between Placement and Payola. *Brandweek* .

Enright, A. (2007, September 15). Inside In-Game Advertising. *Marketing News* , pp. 26-30.

Etcoff, N., Orbach, S., Scott, J., & D'Agostino, H. (2004). *The Real Truth About Beauty: A Global Report.* Dove, A Unilever Beauty Brand.

Fan - or Phony? (n.d.). Retrieved September 7, 2007, from badads.org: http://badads.org/computer/shtml

Feldman, W., Feldman, E., & Goodman, J. (1988). Culture vs. Biology: Children's Attitudes Toward Thinness and Fatness. *Paediatrics* , 81 (2), 191-194.

Ferrel, O., Fraedrich, J., & Ferrell, L. (2002). *Business Ethics Ethical Decision Making and Cases.* Boston: Houghton Mifflin Company.

Fielding, M. (2006, July 15). Dealer Options. *Marketing News* , p. 11.

Fitzgerald, K. (2004, February 9). *Battling for Shoppers in the Aisles.* Retrieved February 17, 2004, from AdAge.com: http://www.adage.com/news.cms?newsId=39742

Fonda, D., & Roston, E. (2004, June 28). Pitching it to Kids. *Time* .

Frazer, J. (2006, November 10). New Meth Ads detail Ugly Reality. *Wyoming Tribune-Eagle* .

Gardner, D. M. (1975, January). Deception in Advertising: A Conceptual Approach. *Journal of Marketing* , pp. 40-46.

Gellman, R. (2006, June 4). The President's Uncreative Identity-Theft Task Force. *DM News* , p. 13.

Gibbons, J. (2000). The Price is Right? In J. Schor, *Do Americans Shop Too Much?* (pp. 49-52). Boston: Beacon Press.

Giordano, C. (2007, March 19). Use Privacy to Build Customer Trust, Loyalty. *DM News* , p. 12.

Godin, S. (1999). *Permission Marketing.* New York: Simon & Schuster.

Goodman, D. (1998, March 2). Special K Drops Thin Models for Health Theme. *Marketing News* , p. 8.

Got Cash? Plastic Gains Ground. (2007, May 20). *St. Cloud Times* , pp. 1E-2E.

Gourley, C. (1999, September). Deception, Puffery, and the Ad Police. *Writing* , p. 6.

Graaf, J. d., Wann, D., & Naylor, T. H. (2001). *Affluenza.* San Francisco: Berrett-Koehler Publishers, Inc.

Grads Boomerang Back to Parents. (2006, October 1). *St. Cloud Times* , pp. 1E-2E.

Grimm, M. (2004, April 5). Is Marketing to Kids Ethical. *Brandweek* .

Hightower, J. (2003, October 28). *Teaching Commercialism.* Retrieved March 1, 2006, from InTheseTimes.com: http://www.inthesetimes.com/comments/php?id=415_0_2_0_C

Hill, A., Draper, E., & Stack, J. (1994). A Weight on Children's Minds: Body Shape Dissatisfaction at 9 Years Old. *International Journal of Obesity* , 18, 183-196.

Hlavinka, K. (2006, October 1). New Trends to Shake Loyalty Strategy Foundation. *Marketing News* , pp. 29-30.

Hoffman, D. A. (2006, October 3). *The Best Puffery Article Ever.* Retrieved October 16, 2007, from worksbepress.com: http://worksbepress.com/cgi/viewcontent.cgi?article=1005&content=Hoffman

Hood, J. (2006). Advertising Benefits Consumers. In L. K. Egendorf, *Advertising: Opposing Viewpoints* (pp. 18-25). Detroit: Thomson Gale.

Horvath, T. (1981). Physical Attractiveness: The Influence of Selected Torso Parameters. *Archives of Sexual Behavior* , pp. 10, 21-24.

Hoyer, W. D., & MacInnis, D. J. (2004). *Consumer Behavior Third Ed.* Boston: Houghton Mifflin Company.

Hyman, M. R., & Tansey, R. (1990, 9). The Ethics of Psychoactive Ads. *Journal of Business Ethics* , pp. 105-114.

(2002). *ID Theft: When Bad Things Happen To Your Good name.* Washington, D.C.: Federal Trade Commision.

Impossibly Thin? (2005, November 11). Retrieved April 11, 2006, from medialit.med.sc.edu: http://medialit.med.sc.edu/impossibly_thin.htm

Is Any Place Sacred? Nah. (n.d.). Retrieved September 7, 2007, from badads.org: http://www.badads.org/misc.shtml

Jade, D. (2002). *Eating Disorders and the Media.* National Centre for Eating Disorders.

Janis, I. L. (1967). Effects of Fear Arousal on Attitude Change. In L. Berkowitz, *Advances in Experimental Psychology* (pp. 166-224). New York: Academic Press.

Kasser, T. (2001). *Research on Materialism and Well-being.* Retrieved September 6, 2007, from www.commercialfreechildhood.org: http://www.commercialfreechildhood.org/2001_summit/t_kasser_summit2001.htm

Kellogg Won't Market Sugary Cereal to Children. (2007, June 14). Retrieved June 14, 2007, from cbsnews.com: http://cbsnews.com/stories/2007/06/14/health/printable2926923.shtml

Kelly, K., & Kulman, L. (2004, September 13). Kid Power. *U.S. News & World Report* .

Kennedy, D. (2004, April 1). Coming of Age in Consumerdom. *American Demographics* .

Kidd, M. (2000, March). White Paper on Self Storage. *Self Storage Association* .

Kilbourne, J. (Director). (2002). *Killing Us Softly 3* [Motion Picture].

Kuipers, H. (1998, March 7). *Anabolic Steroids: Side Effects.* Retrieved April 26, 2006, from www.sportsci.org: http://www.sportsci.org/encyc/anabstereff.html

Kunkel, D., Wilcox, B. L., Cantor, J., Palmer, E., Linn, S., & Dowrick, P. (2004). *Report of the APA Task Force on Advertising and Children, Section: Psychological Issues in the Increasing Commercialization of Childhood.* American Psychological Association.

L.Zurbriggen, E., Collins, R. L., Lamb, S., Roberts, T.-A., Toman, D. L., Ward, L. M., et al. (2007). *Report of the APA Task Force on the Sexualization of Girls.* Washington, D.C.: American Psychological Association.

Lamb, S., & Brown, L. M. (2006). *Packaging Girlhood.* New York: St. Martin's Press.

Lavine, H., Sweeney, D., & Wagner, S. H. (August, 1999). Depicting Women as Sex Objects in Televesion Advertising: Effects on Body Dissatisfaction. *Personality and Social Psychology Bulletin* , 1049-1058.

Leach, W. (1993). *Land of Desire: Merchants, Power, and the Rise of a New American Culture* . New York: Pantheon Books.

Lee, J. (2002, March 21). Welcome to the Database Lounge. *New York Times* , p. G1.

Levitt, H. M. (1997). A Semiotic Understanding of Eating Disorders. *The Journal of treatment and Preventions* , 169-183.

Lewis, K. R. (2005, May 16). Data-Security Breaches Prompt Companies to Rethink 'Pack Rat' Mentality. *Newhouse News Service* .

Linn, S. (2004). *Consuming Kids.* New York: The New Press.

Lucas, A., Beard, C., O'Fallon, W., & Kurland, T. (1991). 50 Year Trends in the Incidence of Anorexia Nervosa in Rochester, Minn.: A Population-based Study. *American Journal of Psychiatry* , pp. 148, 917-922.

Magill, K. (2002, February 11). *Editorial: Interesting, But Useless.* Retrieved February 12, 2002, from iMarketingNews.com: http://www.imarketingnews.com/cgi-bin/artprevbot.cgi?article_id=...

Maloney, M., McGuire, J., Daniels, S., & Specker, B. (1989). Dieting Behavior and Eating Attitudes in Children. *Paediatrics* , 84, 482-489.

152

Marcus, A. (1999). *Body Image Tied to Smoking in Kids*. Merck-Medco Managed Care.

Marketing Terms Dictionary. (2007, 5 22). Retrieved 5 22, 2007, from American Marketing Association MarketingPower.com: http://www.marketingpower.com/mg-dictionary-view1869.php

Marketing to "Tweens" Going Too Far? (2007, May 14). Retrieved May 14, 2007, from cbsnews.com: http://www.cbsnews.com/stories/2007/05/14/earlyshow/living/parenting/printable 2798400

Mazur, A. (1986). U.S. Trends in Feminine Beauty and Overadaptation. *Journal of Sex Research* , 281-301.

McAulay, J. (2006, February 19). Parents, teachers Deal With Trend of Aggressive Advertising to Kids. *Journal-Constitution* .

McNeal, J. U. (1992). *Kids as Customers: A Handbook of Marketing to Children*. New York: Lexington Books.

McWhorter, A. (2003). *An Impossible Fit*. Retrieved March 21, 2006, from www.troubledwith.com: http://www.troubledwith.com/stellent/groups/public///@fotf_troubledwith/docum ents/article...

Media and Eating Disorders. (n.d.). Retrieved April 26, 2006, from raderprograms.com: http://www.raderprograms.com/media.aspx

Meet Generation Plastic. (2007, May 17). Retrieved May 17, 2007, from CBSNews.com: http://www.cbsnews.com/stories/2007/05/17/eveningnews/printable2821916.shtm l

Merriam-Webster Online Dictionar. (2006, February 12). Retrieved February 12, 2006, from www.m-w.com: http://www.m-w.com/dictionary/puffery

Molnar, A. (1996). *Giving Kids the Business: The Commercialization of America's Schools*. Boulder, Colorado: Westview Press.

Moore, F. (2003, August 2-3). There's No Escape. *Bangor Daily News* , p. S6.

More Ad Pitches Could Get Embedded. (2006, May 17). *USA Today* .

Morrison, T. G., Kalin, R., & Morrison, M. A. (2004, Fall). Body-Image Evaluation and Body-Image Among Adolescents: A Test of Sociocultural and Social Comparison Theories. *Adolescence* , pp. 571-592.

Moses, N., Banilivy, M., & Lifshitz, F. (1989). Fear of Obesity Among Adolescent Girls. *Paediatrics* , 83, 393-398.

Mountain Dew. (n.d.). Retrieved July 22, 2007, from mountaindew.com: http://mountaindew.com

Nabiscoworld. (n.d.). Retrieved July 22, 2007, from nabiscoworld.com: http://nabiscoworld.com/

Natenshon, A. (2004). *Parental Influence Takes Precedence Over Barbie and the Media*. Retrieved April 27, 2006, from empoweredparents.com: http://www.empoweredparents.com/1prevention/prevention_09.htm

Neer, K. (n.d.). *How Product Placement Works*. Retrieved September 7, 2007, from money.howstuffworks.com: http://money.howstuffworks.com/product-placement.htm/printable

Neff, J. (2007, September 27). In Its Campaign for real Beauty, Dove Tells Women That They Are As Beautiful As They Are. But the Push is Showing Signs of Aging . *Advertising Age* , p. News 1.

Neimark, J. (n.d.). *Eating Disorders: Men Have Body Image Problems Too*. Retrieved September 7, 2007, from www.healthplace.com: http://www.healthplace.com/communities/Eating_Disorders/men_3.asp

Nestoras, B. (2001, January). Grown-Up Kids (marketing to Generation Y). *Gifts & Decorative Accessories* .

Nicholas, K. (2006, February 3). Kids Marketing Offers a Moving Target. *PR Week* , p. 18.

Nielsen, J. (2004, December 6). *The Most Hated Advertising Techniques* . Retrieved September 7, 2007, from useit.com: http://www.useit.com/alertbox/20041206.html

Ogden, J., & Mundray, K. (1996). The Effect of the Media on Body Satisfaction: The Role of Gender and Size. *European Eating Orders Review* , 4, 171-181.

O'Guinn, T. C., & Shrum, L. C. (1997). The Role of Television in the Construction of Consumer Reality. *Journal of Consumer Research* , 278-294.

Olsen, S. (2007, May 17). *Protecting Kids From Online Food Ads.* Retrieved May 24, 2007, from news.com: http://news.com/2102-1025_3-6184479.html?tag=st.util.print

Orwell, G. (1949). *Nineteen Eighty-Four.* London: Martin Secker and Warburg Limited.

Overview of the Privacy Act of 1974, 2004 Edition. (2004). Retrieved October 8, 2007, from www.usdoj.gov: http://www.usdoj.gov/oip/1974intro.htm

P & G School Programs. (2007, July 10). Retrieved Juky 10, 2007, from www.pgschoolprograms.com: http://www.pgschoolprograms.com

Parker-Pope, T. (n.d.). *Watching Food Ads on TV May Program Kids to Overeat.* Retrieved July 20, 2007, from commercialalert.org: http://www.commercialalert.org/news/archive/2007/07/watching-food-ads-on-tv-may-program-kids-to-overeat

Parks, L. (1998, September 7). Chains Court Teen Shoppers As Cosmetics Customers. *Drug Store News* .

Peake, D. (2007, May 31). Local Rise of the McMansions. *St. Cloud Times* , pp. 1A, 6A.

Phillips, O. (2006, May 1). Where Will Skincare Go Next? *International Cosmetic News* , p. 87.

Pope, H. G., Phillips, K. A., & Olivardia, R. (2000). *The Adonis Complex.* New York: The Free Press.

Preston, I. L. (1996). *The Great American Blow-Up: Puffery in Advertising and Selling.* Madison, Wisconsin: The University of Wisconsin Press.

Privacy Worries Plague E-Biz. (2002, June 4). Retrieved April 11, 2003, from CyberAtlas.internet.com: http://cyberatlas.internet.com/markets/retailing/print/0,,6061_1183061,00.html

Ramirez, J. (2006, July 31). The New Ad Game. *Newsweek* .

Random Sampling: Talk to the Hand. (2004, August 15). *Marketing News* , p. 3.

Real Women Bare Their Real curves. (2005, June 23). Retrieved February 2, 2007, from www.campaignforrealbeauty.com: http://www.campaignforrealbeauty.com/press.asp?id=4563&length=short&section=news

Reardon, K. K. (1991). *Persuasion in Practice.* Newbury Park, California: SAGE Publications.

Research, F. (2007, March 1). Push-me-pull-you. *Marketing News* , p. 4.

Reyes, S. (2006, January 2). Kellogg, Kraft, Knorr Cater to Consumer Needs. *Brandweek* , p. 8.

Reynolds, T. (1999, May 28). *Sharp Rise in Disordered Eating in Fiji Follwos Arrival of Western TV.* Retrieved April 26, 2006, from harvard.edu: http://focus.harvard.edu/1999/May28_1999/soc.html

Richins, M. L. (1991). Social Comparison and the Idealized Images of Advertising. *Journal of Consumer Research* , June, 71-83.

Richins, M. L. (1991, June). Social Comparison and the Idealized Images of Advertising. *Journal of Consumer Research* , pp. 18, 71-83.

Ritzer, G. (1999). *Enchanting a Disenchanted World: Revolutionizing the Means of Consumption.* Thousand Oaks: Pine Forge Press.

Robert O'Hara, J. (2005). *No Place to Hide.* New York: Free Press.

Roberts, D. F., Foehr, U. G., & Rideout, V. (June, 2005 9). *Generation M: Media in the Lives of 8-18 Year-olds.* Retrieved July 12, 2007, from Kaiser Family Foundation: http://www.kff.org/entmedia/7251.cfm

Rotfeld, H. J., & Rotzoll, K. B. (1981). Puffery vs. Fact Claims - Really Different? *Current Issues and Research In Advertising* , 85-103.

Rovell, D. (2004, May 6). *The Tangled Web of Sports and Advertising.* Retrieved May 6, 2004, from espn.com: http://sports.espn.go.com/espn/print?id=1795742&type=story

Rowe, J., & Ruskin, G. (n.d.). *The Parents Bill of Rights: Helping Moms and Dads Fight Commercialism.* Retrieved July 20, 2007, from commercialalert.org: http://www.commercialalert.org/issues/culture/parents-bill-of-rights/the-parents-bill-of-rights-helping-moms-and-dads-fight-commercialism

Rowings, K. (2007, May 18-20). Biggest Threat to Kids Online? . *USA Weekend* , p. 30.

Rules to Restrict Ads Aimed at Youths. (2007, July 19). *St. Cloud Times* , p. 3A.

Schlosser, E. (2002). *Fast Food Nation.* New York: Perennial.

Schor, J. B. (2004). *Born to Buy.* New York: Scribner.

Schor, J. B. (1998). *The Overspent American.* New York: Basic Books.

Schumacher, L. (2007, July 14). Sign Opens Debate. *St. Cloud Times* , p. 1B.

Seattle School Board Approves Comprehensive Suite of Nutrition Policies. (2004, September 3). Retrieved July 20, 2007, from Citizens' Campaign for Commercial Free Schools: http://www.scn.org/cccs/NutritionPressRelease1.htm

Self-Regulatory Program for Children's Advertising. (2006). Retrieved July 20, 2007, from Children's Advertising Review Unit: http://www.caru.org/guidelines/guidelines.pdf

Severson, R. J. (1997). *The Principles of Information Ethics.* Armonk, New York: M.E. Sharpe.

Sharing knowledge is essential in a thriving society. (2007, July 5). Retrieved July 5, 2007, from WRC media: http://www.wrcmedia.com/companies/consumer.asp

Shaw, W. H., & Barry, V. (2007). *Moral Issues in Business Tenth Edition.* Belmont, CA: Thomson Wadsworth.

Sheppard, F. (2005, August 20). *GoFigure: Nike Gets Real in New Women's Ad Campaign.* Retrieved August 23, 2005, from MarketingPower.com: http://www.intellisearchnow.com/mp_pwrpub_view.scml?ppa=7kmst%5D%Beghktppy...

Slater, A., & Tiggermann, M. (2002). A Test of Objectification Theory in Adolescent Girls. *Sex Roles* , pp. 46, 343-349.

Smith, R. A. (2007, February 2). You Should Be so 'Average'. *The Wall Street Journal* , p. B1.

Snoeyenbos, M., Almeder, R., & Humber, J. (2001). *Business Ethics 3rd ed.* . Buffalo, NY: Prometheus Books.

Spam, Spam, Spam, Spam. (n.d.). Retrieved September 7, 2007, from BadAds.org: http://www.badads.org/email/shtml

Spielberg, S. (Director). (2002). *Minority Report* [Motion Picture].

Starek, R. B. (1996). Myths and Half-Truths About Deceptive Advertising. Las Vegas: National Infomercial Marketing Association.

Steinberg, B. (2006, April 18). Look, Up in the Sky! Product Placement! *Wall Street Journal* , p. B1.

Stephen Ambrose, J., & Gelb, J. W. (2004, May). Consumer Privacy Regulation and Litigation in the United States. *The Business lawyer* , pp. 59, 1251.

Study: 70% of Customers Say Companies Know Too Much. (2003, August 21). Retrieved August 21, 2003, from DMNews.com: http://www.dmnews.com/cgi-bin/artprevbot.cgi?article_id=24820

Taylor, B. (2000). The Personal Level. In J. Schor, *Do Americans Shop Too Much?* (pp. 57-62). Boston: Beacon Press.

Taylor, P. W. (1975). *Principles of Ethics: An Introduction to Ethics 2nd ed.* Encino, CA: Dickenson.

Teinowitz, I. (2006, December 4). Pediatricians Demand Cuts in Kids' Advertising; Group Calls on Congress to Halve the Amount of Child-Targeted TV Spots. *Advertising Age* , p. 3.

The Media and Eating Disorders. (n.d.). Retrieved April 24, 2006, from home.comcast.net: http://home.comcast.net/~albhon/media.htm

The Media, Body Image and Eating Disorders. (n.d.). Retrieved March 28, 2006, from nationaleatingdisorders.org: http://www.nationaleatingdisorders.org/p.asp?WebPage_ID=319&Profile_ID=41 166

The Media, Body Image, and Eating Disorders. (2002). Retrieved April 24, 2006, from nationaleatingdisorders.org: http://www.nationaleatingdisorders.org/p,asp?WebPage_ID=319&Profile_ID=41 166

The Radio Age. (2006, January). *National Geographic* , p. 1.

The Skinny on Models. (2007, January 8). *Current Events* , pp. 15, 7.

The World Book Dictionary. (1985). Chicago: World Bok, Inc.

Thibodeau, P. (2002, March 4). Corporate Privacy Credibility Crumbles. *Computerworld* .

This Bust's for You: Police Are Considering Selling Ad Space on Their Patrol Cars. (2002, November 19). Retrieved November 19, 2002 , from twincities.com: http://www.twincities.com/mld/twincities/4556549.htm?template=contentModul..

Thomas G, B., Smith, M. L., Bengen, B., & Johnson, T. G. (1975). Young Viewers Troubling Response to TV Ads. *Harvard Business review* , 109-120.

Thomas, S. G. (2007). *Buy, Buy Baby.* Boston: Hought Mifflin.

Tips for Parenting in a Commercial Culture. (2002, March 6). Retrieved March 6, 2002, from Kids and Commercialism - Center for a New American Dream: http://www.newdream.org/campaign/kids/brochure2.html

U.S. Population Estimtes by Age, Sex, Race, and Hispanic Origin . (2005). Retrieved July 1, 2005, from U.S. Census Bureau: http://www.census.gov.popest/national/asrh/files/NC-EST2005-ALLDATA.txt

Velasquez, M. G. (2006). *Business Ethics 6th ed.* Saddle River, NJ: Prentice Hall.

Waxman, R. G. (1998). Boys and Body Image. *San Diego Parent Magazine* .

Weasel Words. (1999, September). *Writing* , pp. 1, 5.

Web Site Lets 1 Kid's Trash Be Another Kid's Treasure. (2006, December 23). *St. Cloud Times* , p. 4A.

Weight Standards Recommended for NYC Fashion Models. (2007, January 31). Retrieved April 17, 2007, from www.cbc.ca: http://www.cbc.ca/news/story/2007/01/31/model-guidelines.html

What Do Houston Kids Eat? Parent Are Watching. (2006, February 21). *St. Cloud Times* , p. 7A.

Wheele, T., & Gleason, T. (1995). Photography or Photofiction?: An Ethical Protocol for the Digital Age. *Visual Communication Quarterly* , 8-12.

Whitney, D. (2005, February 21). For Kids TV, Every Day is Saturday. *Advertising Age* , p. S10.

Women's Health. (n.d.). Retrieved April 27, 2006, from Taftcollege.ca: http://www.taft.cc.ca.us/newTC/StudentServices/health/women_issues.htm

Wood, D. J. (2005, December 19). Ad Issues to Watch for in '06. *Advertising Age*

Word, R. (2006, September 15). Motorists Sue Over Auto Registration Ads. *Marketing News* , p. 59.

Zoll, M. H. (2000, April 5). *Psychologists Challenge the Ethics of Marketing to Children.* Retrieved March 1, 2006, from MediaChannel.org: http://www.mediachannel.org/originals/kidsell.shtml

Zukin, S. (2004). *Point of Purchase: How Shopping Changed American Culture.* New York: Routledge.

Subject Index

"Inverted U" model, 16
AMA Code of Conduct, 6
American Academy of Pediatrics, 40, 52, 149
American Marketing Association, 1, 6, 7, 113, 115, 153
American Society of Plastic Surgeons, 77
anorexia nervosa, 77, 82
bigorexia, 83
body dissatisfaction, 72, 74, 75, 77, 81
body image, 72, 75, 77, 78, 80, 82, 84, 87
body shape, 78, 79
Business ethics, 2, 7
Cable Communications Policy Act of 1984, 98
Campaign for Real Beauty, 87
CAN-SPAM Act of 2003, 97
Channel One, 44
Children's Advertising Review Unit, 55
children's market, 37, 38
Children's Online Privacy Protection Act, 3, 48, 96
code of ethics, 6
Code of Fair Information practices, 99
Cognitive theories, 80
Commercial Alert, 31, 52
communications model, 22
consumer attitudes, 12
consumer data, 10, 92, 97
consumer debt, 65, 66
consumer privacy issues, 94
consumer private information, 94
Consumptionism, 57
cookies, 94
Cosmetic surgery, 77

Council of Fashion Designers of America, 86, 144
Council on Economic Priorities, 68
cultural beauty ideals, 77
data security system, 94
database, 94
deceptive advertising, 10, 104, 105
diet industry, 78
digital manipulation, 79
Digital retouching, 79
Direct Marketing Association, 35, 53, 92, 99
Discretionary Products Matrix, 59
disposable income, 65
eating disorders, 71, 72, 75, 77, 78, 82, 86, 144
emotional marketing, 13
ethical decision, 3
ethical issues, 3, 9, 13, 40, 113, 119
Ethical issues, 4
ethical marketing issues, 1, 10
Ethical responsibilities, 2
Ethics Resource Center, 1
Expectancy-value models, 14
Fair and Accurate Credit Transactions Act of 2003, 97
FCC, 27, 39
fear appeal, 11, 12, 13, 14, 17
Federal Communications Commission, 39
Federal Sentencing Guidelines for Organizations, 3
Federal Trade Commission, 39, 53, 97, 99, 104, 123
Floorgraphics, 33
free will, 5, 61, 112
FTC, 27, 39, 53, 99, 104, 105, 135
Generation Y, 37, 155
household debt, 65
idealized bodies, 76

161